Functional Swift

Chris Eidhof, Florian Kugler, Wouter Swierstra

Version 2.0 (December 2015)

For more books and articles visit us at http://objc.io
Email: mail@objc.io
Twitter: @obcio

Introduction

Why write this book? There is plenty of documentation on Swift readily available from Apple, and there are many more books on the way. Why does the world need yet another book on yet another programming language?

This book tries to teach you to think *functionally*. We believe that Swift has the right language features to teach you how to write *functional programs*. But what makes a program functional? And why bother learning about this in the first place?

It is hard to give a precise definition of functional programming — in the same way, it is hard to give a precise definition of object-oriented programming, or any other programming paradigm for that matter. Instead, we will try to focus on some of the *qualities* that we believe well-designed functional programs in Swift should exhibit:

→ **Modularity:** Rather than thinking of a program as a sequence of assignments and method calls, functional programmers emphasize that each program can be repeatedly broken into smaller and smaller pieces, and all these pieces can be assembled using function application to define a complete program. Of course, this decomposition of a large program into smaller pieces only works if we can avoid sharing state between the individual components. This brings us to our next point.

→ **A Careful Treatment of Mutable State:** Functional programming is sometimes (half-jokingly) referred to as 'value-oriented programming.' Object-oriented programming focuses on the design of classes and objects, each with their own encapsulated state. Functional programming, on the other hand, emphasizes the importance of programming with values, free of mutable state or other side effects. By avoiding mutable state, functional programs can be more easily combined than their imperative or object-oriented counterparts.

→ **Types:** Finally, a well-designed functional program makes careful use of *types*. More than anything else, a careful choice of the types of your data and functions will help structure your code. Swift has a powerful type system that, when used effectively, can make your code both safer and more robust.

We feel these are the key insights that Swift programmers may learn from the functional programming community. Throughout this book, we will illustrate each of these points with many examples and case studies.

In our experience, learning to think functionally is not easy. It challenges the way we've been trained to decompose problems. For programmers who are used to writing **for** loops, recursion can be confusing; the lack of assignment statements and global state is crippling; and closures, generics, higher-order functions, and monads are just plain weird.

Throughout this book, we will assume that you have previous programming experience in Objective-C (or some other object-oriented language). We won't cover Swift basics or teach you to set up your first Xcode project, but we will try to refer to existing Apple documentation when appropriate. You should be comfortable reading Swift programs and familiar with common programming concepts, such as classes, methods, and variables. If you've only just started to learn to program, this may not be the right book for you.

In this book, we want to demystify functional programming and dispel some of the prejudices people may have against it. You don't need to have a PhD in mathematics to use these ideas to improve your code! Functional programming is not the *only* way to program in Swift. Instead, we believe that learning about functional programming adds an important new tool to your toolbox that will make you a better developer in any language.

Sample Code

You can find all the sample code from this book in our GitHub repository[1]. This repository contains playgrounds for some chapters, and swift files and an OS X project for the others.

Updates to the Book

As Swift evolves, we'll continue to make updates and enhancements to this book. Should you encounter any mistakes, or if you would like to send any other kind of feedback our way, please file an issue in our GitHub repository[2].

1 https://github.com/objcio/functional-swift
2 https://github.com/objcio/functional-swift

Acknowledgements

We'd like to thank the numerous people who helped shape this book. We wanted to explicitly mention some of them:

Natalye Childress is our copy editor. She has provided invaluable feedback, not only making sure the language is correct and consistent, but also making sure things are understandable.

Sarah Lincoln designed the cover and the layout of the book.

Wouter would like to thank *Utrecht University* for letting him take time to work on this book.

We would like to thank the beta readers for their feedback during the writing of this book (listed in alphabetical order):

Adrian Kosmaczewski, Alexander Altman, Andrew Halls, Bang Jun-young, Daniel Eggert, Daniel Steinberg, David Hart, David Owens II, Eugene Dorfman, f-dz-v, Henry Stamerjohann, J Bucaran, Jamie Forrest, Jaromir Siska, Jason Larsen, Jesse Armand, John Gallagher, Kaan Dedeoglu, Kare Morstol, Kiel Gillard, Kristopher Johnson, Matteo Piombo, Nicholas Outram, Ole Begemann, Rob Napier, Ronald Mannak, Sam Isaacson, Ssu Jen Lu, Stephen Horne, TJ, Terry Lewis, Tim Brooks, Vadim Shpakovski.

Chris, Florian, and Wouter

Thinking
Functionally

Functions in Swift are *first-class values,* i.e. functions may be passed as arguments to other functions, and functions may return new functions. This idea may seem strange if you're used to working with simple types, such as integers, booleans, or structs. In this chapter, we will try to explain why first-class functions are useful and provide our first example of functional programming in action.

Example: Battleship

We will introduce first-class functions using a small example: a non-trivial function that you might need to implement if you were writing a Battleship-like game. The problem we'll look at boils down to determining whether or not a given point is in range, without being too close to friendly ships or to us.

As a first approximation, you might write a very simple function that checks whether or not a point is in range. For the sake of simplicity, we will assume that our ship is located at the origin. We can visualize the region we want to describe in Figure 2.1:

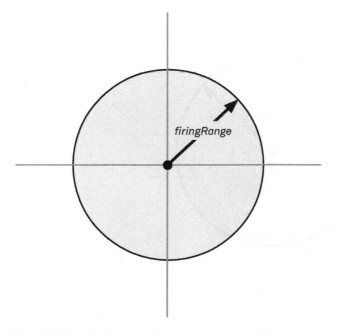

Figure 2.1: The points in range of a ship located at the origin

First, we'll define two types, Distance and Position:

```
typealias Distance = Double

struct Position {
    var x: Double
    var y: Double
}
```

Now we add a function to Position, inRange(_:), which checks that a point is in the grey area in Figure 2.1. Using some basic geometry, we can write this function as follows:

```
extension Position {
    func inRange(range: Distance) -> Bool {
        return sqrt(x * x + y * y) <= range
    }
}
```

This works fine, if you assume that we are always located at the origin. But suppose the ship may be at a location other than the origin. We can update our visualization in Figure 2.2:

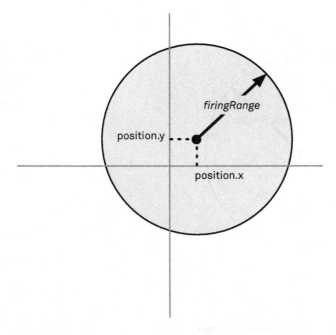

Figure 2.2: Allowing the ship to have its own position

To account for this, we introduce a Ship struct that has a position property:

```
struct Ship {
    var position:  Position
    var firingRange: Distance
    var unsafeRange: Distance
}
```

For now, just ignore the additional property, unsafeRange. We'll come back to this in a bit.

We extend the Ship struct with a function, canEngageShip(_:), which allows us to test if another ship is in range, irrespective of whether we're located at the origin or at any other position:

```
extension Ship {
    func canEngageShip(target: Ship) -> Bool {
        let dx = target.position.x - position.x
        let dy = target.position.y - position.y
        let targetDistance = sqrt(dx * dx + dy * dy)
        return targetDistance <= firingRange
    }
}
```

But now you realize that you also want to avoid targeting ships if they are too close to you. We can update our visualization to illustrate the new situation in Figure 2.3, where we want to target only those enemies that are at least unsafeRange away from our current position:

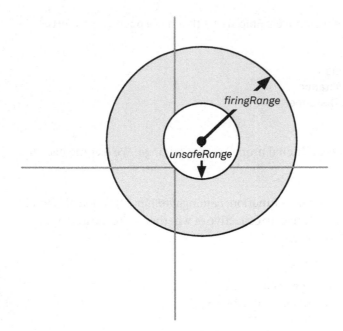

Figure 2.3: Avoiding engaging enemies too close to the ship

As a result, we need to modify our code again, making use of the unsafeRange property:

```
extension Ship {
    func canSafelyEngageShip(target: Ship) -> Bool {
        let dx = target.position.x - position.x
        let dy = target.position.y - position.y
        let targetDistance = sqrt(dx * dx + dy * dy)
        return targetDistance <= firingRange && targetDistance > unsafeRange
    }
}
```

Finally, you also need to avoid targeting ships that are too close to one of your other ships. Once again, we can visualize this in Figure 2.4:

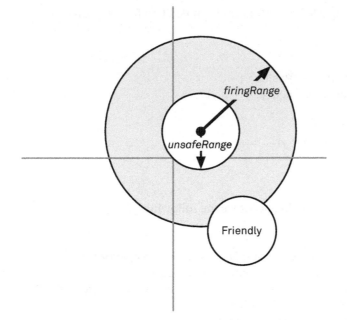

Figure 2.4: Avoiding engaging targets too close to friendly ships

Correspondingly, we can add a further argument that represents the location of a friendly ship to our canSafelyEngageShip(_:) function:

```
extension Ship {
    func canSafelyEngageShip1(target: Ship, friendly: Ship) -> Bool {
        let dx = target.position.x - position.x
        let dy = target.position.y - position.y
        let targetDistance = sqrt(dx * dx + dy * dy)
        let friendlyDx = friendly.position.x - target.position.x
        let friendlyDy = friendly.position.y - target.position.y
        let friendlyDistance = sqrt(friendlyDx * friendlyDx +
            friendlyDy * friendlyDy)
        return targetDistance <= firingRange
            && targetDistance > unsafeRange
            && (friendlyDistance > unsafeRange)
    }
}
```

As this code evolves, it becomes harder and harder to maintain. This method expresses a complicated calculation in one big lump of code. We can clean this code up a bit by adding two helper functions on Position for the geometric calculations:

```
extension Position {
    func minus(p: Position) -> Position {
        return Position(x:  x - p.x,  y:  y - p.y)
    }
    var length: Double {
        return sqrt(x * x + y * y)
    }
}
```

Using those helpers, the function becomes the following:

```
extension Ship {
    func canSafelyEngageShip2(target: Ship, friendly: Ship) -> Bool {
        let  targetDistance = target.position.minus(position).length
        let  friendlyDistance = friendly.position.minus(target.position).length
        return targetDistance <= firingRange
            && targetDistance > unsafeRange
            && (friendlyDistance > unsafeRange)
    }
}
```

This is already much more readable, but we want to go one step further and take a more declarative route to specifying the problem at hand.

First-Class Functions

In the current incarnation of the canSafelyEngageShip function, its behavior is encoded in the combination of boolean conditions the return value is comprised of. While it's not too hard to figure out what this function does in this simple case, we want to have a solution that's more modular.

We already introduced helper functions on Position to clean up the code for the geometric calculations. In a similar fashion, we'll now add functions to test whether a region contains a point in a more declarative manner.

The original problem boiled down to defining a function that determined when a point was in range or not. The type of such a function would be something like this:

```
func pointInRange(point: Position) -> Bool {
    // Implement method here
}
```

The type of this function is going to be so important that we're going to give it a separate name:

```
typealias Region = Position -> Bool
```

From now on, the Region type will refer to functions transforming a Position to a Bool. This isn't strictly necessary, but it can make some of the type signatures that we'll see below a bit easier to digest.

Instead of defining an object or struct to represent regions, we represent a region by a *function* that determines if a given point is in the region or not. If you're not used to functional programming, this may seem strange, but remember: functions in Swift are first-class values! We consciously chose the name Region for this type, rather than something like CheckInRegion or RegionBlock. These names suggest that they denote a function type, yet the key philosophy underlying *functional programming* is that functions are values, no different from structs, integers, or booleans — using a separate naming convention for functions would violate this philosophy.

We will now write several functions that create, manipulate, and combine regions.

The first region we define is a circle, centered around the origin:

```
func circle(radius: Distance) -> Region {
    return { point in point.length <= radius }
}
```

Of course, not all circles are centered around the origin. We could add more arguments to the circle function to account for this. To compute a circle that's centered around a certain position, we just add another argument representing the circle's center and make sure to account for this value when computing the new region:

```
func circle2(radius: Distance, center: Position) -> Region {
    return { point in point.minus(center).length <= radius }
}
```

However, if we we want to make the same change to more primitives (for example, imagine we not only had circles, but also rectangles or other shapes), we might need to duplicate this code. A more functional approach is to write a *region transformer* instead. This function shifts a region by a certain offset:

```
func shift(region: Region, offset: Position) -> Region {
    return { point in region(point.minus(offset)) }
}
```

The call shift(region, offset: offset) moves the region to the right and up by offset.x and offset.y, respectively. We need to return a Region, which is a function from a point to a boolean value. To do this, we start writing another closure, introducing the point we need to check. From this point, we compute a new point by subtracting the offset. Finally, we check that this new point is in the *original* region by passing it as an argument to the region function.

This is one of the core concepts of functional programming: rather than creating increasingly complicated functions such as circle2, we have written a function, shift(_:offset:), that modifies another function. For example, a circle that's centered at (5, 5) and has a radius of 10 can now be expressed like this:

```
shift(circle(10), offset: Position(x: 5, y: 5))
```

There are lots of other ways to transform existing regions. For instance, we may want to define a new region by inverting a region. The resulting region consists of all the points outside the original region:

```
func invert(region: Region) -> Region {
    return { point in !region(point) }
}
```

We can also write functions that combine existing regions into larger, complex regions. For instance, these two functions take the points that are in *both* argument regions or *either* argument region, respectively:

```
func intersection(region1: Region, _ region2: Region) -> Region {
    return { point in region1(point) && region2(point) }
}

func union(region1: Region, _ region2: Region) -> Region {
    return { point in region1(point) || region2(point) }
}
```

Of course, we can use these functions to define even richer regions. The difference function takes two regions as argument — the original region and the region to be subtracted — and constructs a new region function for all points that are in the first, but not in the second, region:

```
func difference(region: Region, minus: Region) -> Region {
    return intersection(region, invert(minus))
}
```

This example shows how Swift lets you compute and pass around functions no differently than you would integers or booleans. This enables us to write small primitives (such as circle) and to build a series of functions on top of these primitives. Each of these functions modifies or combines regions into new regions. Instead of writing complex functions to solve a very specific problem, we can now use many small functions that can be assembled to solve a wide variety of problems.

Now let's turn our attention back to our original example. With this small library in place, we can refactor the complicated canSafelyEngageShip(_:friendly:) function as follows:

```
extension Ship {
    func canSafelyEngageShip(target: Ship, friendly: Ship) -> Bool {
        let rangeRegion = difference(circle(firingRange),
            minus: circle(unsafeRange))
        let firingRegion = shift(rangeRegion, offset: position)
        let friendlyRegion = shift(circle(unsafeRange),
            offset: friendly.position)
        let resultRegion = difference(firingRegion, minus: friendlyRegion)
        return resultRegion(target.position)
    }
}
```

This code defines two regions: firingRegion and friendlyRegion. The region that we're interested in is computed by taking the difference between these regions. By applying this region to the target ship's position, we can compute the desired boolean.

Compared to the original canSafelyEngageShip1(_:friendly:) function, the refactored method provides a more *declarative* solution to the same problem by using the Region functions. We argue that the latter version is easier to understand because the solution is *compositional*. You can study each of its constituent regions, such as firingRegion and friendlyRegion, and see how these are assembled to solve the original problem. The original, monolithic function, on the other hand, mixes the description of the constituent regions and the calculations needed to describe them. Separating these concerns by defining the helper functions we presented previously increases the compositionality and legibility of complex regions.

Having first-class functions is essential for this to work. Objective-C also supports first-class functions, or *blocks*. It can, unfortunately, be quite cumbersome to work with blocks. Part of this is a syntax issue: both the declaration of a block and the type of a block are not as straightforward as their Swift counterparts. In later chapters, we will also see how generics make first-class functions even more powerful, going beyond what is easy to achieve with blocks in Objective-C.

The way we've defined the Region type does have its disadvantages. Here we have chosen to define the Region type as a simple type alias for Position -> Bool functions. Instead, we could have chosen to define a struct containing a single function:

```
struct Region {
    let lookup: Position -> Bool
}
```

Instead of the functions operating on our original Region type, we could then define similar functions as extensions to this struct. And instead of assembling complex regions by passing them to functions, we could then repeatedly transform a region by calling these methods:

```
rangeRegion.shift(ownPosition).difference(friendlyRegion)
```

The latter approach has the advantage of requiring fewer parentheses. Furthermore, Xcode's autocompletion can be invaluable when assembling complex regions in this fashion. For the sake of presentation, however, we have chosen to use a simple type alias to highlight how higher-order functions can be used in Swift.

Furthermore, it is worth pointing out that we cannot inspect *how* a region was constructed: is it composed of smaller regions? Or is it simply a circle around the origin? The only thing we can do is to check whether a given point is within a region or not. If we want to visualize a region, we would have to sample enough points to generate a (black and white) bitmap.

In a later chapter, we will sketch an alternative design that will allow you to answer these questions.

Type-Driven Development

In the introduction, we mentioned how functional programs take the application of functions to arguments as the canonical way to assemble bigger programs. In this chapter, we have seen a concrete example of this functional design methodology. We have defined a series of functions for describing regions. Each of these functions is not very powerful by itself. Yet together, they can describe complex regions that you wouldn't want to write from scratch.

The solution is simple and elegant. It is quite different from what you might write if you had naively refactored the canSafelyEngageShip1(_:friendly:) function into separate methods. The crucial design decision we made was *how* to define regions. Once we chose the Region type, all the other definitions followed naturally. The moral of the example is **choose your types carefully**. More than anything else, types guide the development process.

Notes

The code presented here is inspired by the Haskell solution to a problem posed by the United States Advanced Research Projects Agency (ARPA) by Hudak and Jones (1994).

Objective-C added support for first-class functions with the addition of blocks: you can use functions and closures as parameters and easily define them inline. However, working with them is not nearly as convenient in Objective-C as it is in Swift, even though they're semantically equivalent.

Historically, the idea of first-class functions can be traced as far back as Church's lambda calculus (Church 1941; Barendregt 1984). Since then, the concept has made its way into numerous (functional) programming languages, including Haskell, OCaml, Standard ML, Scala, and F#.

Case Study: Wrapping Core Image

The previous chapter introduced the concept of *higher-order functions* and showed how functions can be passed as arguments to other functions. However, the example used there may seem far removed from the 'real' code that you write on a daily basis. In this chapter, we will show how to use higher-order functions to write a small, functional wrapper around an existing, object-oriented API.

Core Image is a powerful image processing framework, but its API can be a bit clunky to use at times. The Core Image API is loosely typed — image filters are configured using key-value coding. It is all too easy to make mistakes in the type or name of arguments, which can result in runtime errors. The new API we develop will be safe and modular, exploiting *types* to guarantee the absence of such runtime errors.

Don't worry if you're unfamiliar with Core Image or cannot understand all the details of the code fragments in this chapter. The goal isn't to build a complete wrapper around Core Image, but instead to illustrate how concepts from functional programming, such as higher-order functions, can be applied in production code.

The Filter Type

One of the key classes in Core Image is the CIFilter class, which is used to create image filters. When you instantiate a CIFilter object, you (almost) always provide an input image via the kCIInputImageKey key, and then retrieve the filtered result via the kCIOutputImageKey key. Then you can use this result as input for the next filter.

In the API we will develop in this chapter, we'll try to encapsulate the exact details of these key-value pairs and present a safe, strongly typed API to our users. We define our own Filter type as a function that takes an image as its parameter and returns a new image:

```
typealias Filter = CIImage -> CIImage
```

This is the base type that we are going to build upon.

Building Filters

Now that we have the Filter type defined, we can start defining functions that build specific filters. These are convenience functions that take the parameters needed for a specific filter and construct a value of type Filter. These functions will all have the following general shape:

```
func myFilter(/* parameters */) -> Filter
```

Blur

Let's define our first simple filters. The Gaussian blur filter only has the blur radius as its parameter:

```
func blur(radius: Double) -> Filter {
    return { image in
        let parameters = [
            kCIInputRadiusKey: radius,
            kCIInputImageKey: image
        ]
        guard let filter = CIFilter(name: "CIGaussianBlur",
            withInputParameters: parameters) else { fatalError() }
        guard let outputImage = filter.outputImage else { fatalError() }
        return outputImage
    }
}
```

That's all there is to it. The blur function returns a function that takes an argument image of type CIImage and returns a new image (**return** filter .outputImage). Because of this, the return value of the blur function conforms to the Filter type we defined previously as CIImage -> CIImage.

This example is just a thin wrapper around a filter that already exists in Core Image. We can use the same pattern over and over again to create our own filter functions.

Color Overlay

Let's define a filter that overlays an image with a solid color of our choice. Core Image doesn't have such a filter by default, but we can, of course, compose it from existing filters.

The two building blocks we're going to use for this are the color generator filter (CIConstantColorGenerator) and the source-over compositing filter (CISourceOverCompositing). Let's first define a filter to generate a constant color plane:

```
func colorGenerator(color: NSColor) -> Filter {
    return { _ in
        guard let c = CIColor(color: color) else { fatalError() }
        let parameters = [kCIInputColorKey: c]
        guard let filter = CIFilter(name: "CIConstantColorGenerator",
            withInputParameters: parameters) else { fatalError() }
        guard let outputImage = filter.outputImage else { fatalError() }
        return outputImage
    }
}
```

This looks very similar to the blur filter we've defined above, with one notable difference: the constant color generator filter does not inspect its input image. Therefore, we don't need to name the image parameter in the function being returned. Instead, we use an unnamed parameter, _, to emphasize that the image argument to the filter we are defining is ignored.

Next, we're going to define the composite filter:

```
func compositeSourceOver(overlay: CIImage) -> Filter {
    return { image in
        let parameters = [
            kCIInputBackgroundImageKey: image,
            kCIInputImageKey: overlay
        ]
        guard let filter = CIFilter(name: "CISourceOverCompositing",
            withInputParameters: parameters) else { fatalError() }
        guard let outputImage = filter.outputImage else { fatalError() }
        let cropRect = image.extent
        return outputImage.imageByCroppingToRect(cropRect)
    }
}
```

Here we crop the output image to the size of the input image. This is not strictly necessary, and it depends on how we want the filter to behave. However, this choice works well in the examples we will cover.

Finally, we combine these two filters to create our color overlay filter:

```swift
func colorOverlay(color: NSColor) -> Filter {
    return { image in
        let overlay = colorGenerator(color)(image)
        return compositeSourceOver(overlay)(image)
    }
}
```

Once again, we return a function that takes an image parameter as its argument. The colorOverlay starts by calling the colorGenerator filter. The colorGenerator filter requires a color as its argument and returns a filter, hence the code snippet colorGenerator(color) has type Filter. The Filter type, however, is itself a function from CIImage to CIImage; we can pass an *additional* argument of type CIImage to colorGenerator(color) to compute a new overlay CIImage. This is exactly what happens in the definition of overlay — we create a filter using the colorGenerator function and pass the image argument to this filter to create a new image. Similarly, the value returned, compositeSourceOver(overlay)(image), consists of a filter, compositeSourceOver(overlay), being constructed and subsequently applied to the image argument.

Composing Filters

Now that we have a blur and a color overlay filter defined, we can put them to use on an actual image in a combined way: first we blur the image, and then we put a red overlay on top. Let's load an image to work on:

```swift
let url = NSURL(string: "http://www.objc.io/images/covers/16.jpg")!
let image = CIImage(contentsOfURL: url)!
```

Now we can apply both filters to these by chaining them together:

```swift
let blurRadius = 5.0
let overlayColor = NSColor.redColor().colorWithAlphaComponent(0.2)
let blurredImage = blur(blurRadius)(image)
let overlaidImage = colorOverlay(overlayColor)(blurredImage)
```

Once again, we assemble images by creating a filter, such as blur(blurRadius), and applying the resulting filter to an image.

Function Composition

Of course, we could simply combine the two filter calls in the above code in a single expression:

```
let result = colorOverlay(overlayColor)(blur(blurRadius)(image))
```

However, this becomes unreadable very quickly with all these parentheses involved. A nicer way to do this is to compose filters by defining a custom operator for filter composition. To do so, we'll start by defining a function that composes filters:

```
func composeFilters(filter1: Filter, _ filter2 : Filter) -> Filter {
    return { image in filter2 ( filter1 (image)) }
}
```

The composeFilters function takes two argument filters and defines a new filter. This composite filter expects an argument image of type CIImage and passes it through both filter1 and filter2, respectively. We can use function composition to define our own composite filter, like this:

```
let myFilter1 = composeFilters(blur(blurRadius), colorOverlay(overlayColor))
let result1 = myFilter1(image)
```

We can go one step further to make this even more readable, by introducing an operator for filter composition. Granted, defining your own operators all over the place doesn't necessarily contribute to the readability of your code. However, filter composition is a recurring task in an image processing library, so it makes a lot of sense:

```
infix operator >>> { associativity left }
```

```
func >>> ( filter1 : Filter, filter2 : Filter) -> Filter {
    return { image in filter2 ( filter1 (image)) }
}
```

Now we can use the >>> operator in the same way we used composeFilters before:

```
let myFilter2 = blur(blurRadius) >>> colorOverlay(overlayColor)
let result2 = myFilter2(image)
```

Since we have defined the >>> operator as being left-associative we can read the filters that are applied to an image from left to right — like Unix pipes.

The filter composition operation that we have defined is an example of *function composition*. In mathematics, the composition of the two functions f and g, sometimes written f ◻ g, defines a new function mapping an input x to $f(g(x))$. With the exception of the order, this is precisely what our >>> operator does: it passes an argument image through its two constituent filters.

Theoretical Background: Currying

In this chapter, we've seen that there are two ways to define a function that takes two arguments. The first style is familiar to most programmers:

```
func add1(x: Int, _ y: Int) -> Int {
    return x + y
}
```

The add1 function takes two integer arguments and returns their sum. In Swift, however, we can also define another version of the same function:

```
func add2(x: Int) -> (Int -> Int) {
    return { y in return x + y }
}
```

Here, the function add2 takes one argument, x, and returns a *closure*, expecting a second argument, y. These two add functions must be invoked differently:

```
add1(1, 2)
add2(1)(2)
```

3

In the first case, we pass both arguments to add1 at the same time; in the second case, we first pass the first argument, 1, which returns a function, which we then apply to the second argument, 2. Both versions are equivalent: we can define add1 in terms of add2, and vice versa.

In Swift, we can even leave out one of the return statements and some of the parentheses in the type signature of add2, and write:

```
func add2(x: Int) -> Int -> Int {
    return { y in x + y }
}
```

The function arrow, ->, associates to the right. That is to say, you can read the type A -> B -> C as A -> (B -> C). Throughout this book, however, we will typically introduce a type alias for functional types (as we did for the Region and Filter types), or write explicit parentheses.

The add1 and add2 examples show how we can always transform a function that expects multiple arguments into a series of functions that each expect one argument. This process is referred to as *currying*, named after the logician Haskell Curry; we say that add2 is the *curried* version of add1.

There is a third way to curry functions in Swift. Instead of constructing the closure explicitly, as we did in the definition of add2, we can also define a curried version of add1 as follows:

```
func add3(x: Int)(_ y: Int) -> Int {
    return x + y
}
```

Here we have listed the arguments that add3 expects, one after the other, each surrounded by its own parentheses. By specifying the second argument as an underscore, we can call it without naming the second argument:

```
add3(1)(2)
```

```
3
```

So why is currying interesting? As we have seen in this book thus far, there are scenarios where you want to pass functions as arguments to other functions. If we have *uncurried* functions, like add1, we can only apply a function to *both* its arguments. On the other hand, for a *curried* function, like add2, we have a choice: we can apply it to one *or* two arguments. The functions for creating filters that we have defined in this chapter have all been curried — they all expected an additional image argument. By writing our filters in this style, we were able to compose them easily using the >>> operator. Had we instead worked with *uncurried* versions of the same functions, it still would have been possible to write the same filters. These filters, however, would all have a slightly different type, depending on the arguments they expect. As a result, it would be much harder to define a single composition operator for the many different types that our filters might have.

Discussion

This example illustrates, once again, how we break complex code into small pieces, which can all be reassembled using function application. The goal of this chapter was not to define a complete API around Core Image, but instead to sketch out how higher-order functions and function composition can be used in a more practical case study.

Why go through all this effort? It's true that the Core Image API is already mature and provides all the functionality you might need. But in spite of this, we believe there are several advantages to the API designed in this chapter:

→ **Safety** — using the API we have sketched, it is almost impossible to create runtime errors arising from undefined keys or failed casts.

→ **Modularity** — it is easy to compose filters using the >>> operator. Doing so allows you to tease apart complex filters into smaller, simpler, reusable components. Additionally, composed filters have the exact same type as their building blocks, so you can use them interchangeably.

→ **Clarity** — even if you have never used Core Image, you should be able to assemble simple filters using the functions we have defined. To access the results, you don't need to know about special dictionary keys, such as kCIOutputImageKey, or worry about initializing certain keys, such as kCIInputImageKey or kCIInputRadiusKey. From the types alone, you can almost figure out how to use the API, even without further documentation.

Our API presents a series of functions that can be used to define and compose filters. Any filters that you define are safe to use and reuse. Each filter can be tested and understood in isolation. We believe these are compelling reasons to favor the design sketched here over the original Core Image API.

Map, Filter, Reduce

Functions that take functions as arguments are sometimes called *higher-order* functions. In this chapter, we will tour some of the higher-order functions on arrays from the Swift standard library. By doing so, we will introduce Swift's *generics* and show how to assemble complex computations on arrays.

Introducing Generics

Suppose we need to write a function that, given an array of integers, computes a new array, where every integer in the original array has been incremented by one. Such a function is easy to write using a single **for** loop:

```
func incrementArray(xs: [Int]) -> [Int] {
    var result: [Int] = []
    for x in xs {
        result.append(x + 1)
    }
    return result
}
```

Now suppose we also need a function that computes a new array, where every element in the argument array has been doubled. This is also easy to do using a **for** loop:

```
func doubleArray1(xs: [Int]) -> [Int] {
    var result: [Int] = []
    for x in xs {
        result.append(x * 2)
    }
    return result
}
```

Both of these functions share a lot of code. Can we abstract over the differences and write a single, more general function that captures this pattern? Such a function would need a second argument that takes a function, which computes a new integer from an individual element of the array:

```
func computeIntArray(xs: [Int], transform: Int -> Int) -> [Int] {
    var result: [Int] = []
    for x in xs {
        result.append(transform(x))
    }
    return result
}
```

Now we can pass different arguments, depending on how we want to compute a new array from the old array. The doubleArray and incrementArray functions become one-liners that call computeIntArray:

```
func doubleArray2(xs: [Int]) -> [Int] {
    return computeIntArray(xs) { x in x * 2 }
}
```

This code is still not as flexible as it could be. Suppose we want to compute a new array of booleans, describing whether the numbers in the original array were even or not. We might try to write something like this:

```
func isEvenArray(xs: [Int]) -> [Bool] {
    computeIntArray(xs) { x in x % 2 == 0 }
}
```

Unfortunately, this code gives a type error. The problem is that our computeIntArray function takes an argument of type Int -> Int, that is, a function that returns an integer. In the definition of isEvenArray, we are passing an argument of type Int -> Bool, which causes the type error.

How should we solve this? One thing we *could* do is define a new version of computeIntArray that takes a function argument of type Int -> Bool. That might look something like this:

```
func computeBoolArray(xs: [Int], transform: Int -> Bool) -> [Bool] {
    var result: [Bool] = []
    for x in xs {
        result.append(transform(x))
    }
    return result
}
```

This doesn't scale very well though. What if we need to compute a String next? Do we need to define yet another higher-order function, expecting an argument of type Int -> String?

Luckily, there is a solution to this problem: we can use generics. The definitions of computeBoolArray and computeIntArray are identical; the only difference is in the *type signature*. If we were to define another version, computeStringArray, the body of the function would be the same again. In fact, the same code will work for *any* type. What we really want to do is write a single generic function that will work for every possible type:

```
func genericComputeArray1<T>(xs: [Int], transform: Int -> T) -> [T] {
    var result: [T] = []
    for x in xs {
        result.append(transform(x))
    }
    return result
}
```

The most interesting thing about this piece of code is its type signature. To understand this type signature, it may help you to think of genericComputeArray<T> as a family of functions. Each choice of the *type* parameter T determines a new function. This function takes an array of integers and a function of type Int -> T as arguments, and returns an array of type [T].

We can generalize this function even further. There is no reason for it to operate exclusively on input arrays of type [Int]. Abstracting over this yields the following type signature:

```
func map<Element, T>(xs: [Element], transform: Element -> T) -> [T] {
    var result: [T] = []
    for x in xs {
        result.append(transform(x))
    }
    return result
}
```

Here we have written a function, map, that is generic in two dimensions: for any array of Elements and function transform: Element -> T, it will produce a new array of Ts. This map function is even more generic than the genericComputeArray function we saw earlier. In fact, we can define genericComputeArray in terms of map:

```
func genericComputeArray2<T>(xs: [Int], transform: Int -> T) -> [T] {
    return map(xs, transform: transform)
}
```

Once again, the definition of the function is not that interesting: given two arguments, xs and transform, apply map to (xs, transform), and return the result. The types are the most interesting thing about this definition. The genericComputeArray(_:transform:) is an instance of the map function, only it has a more specific type.

Instead of defining a top-level map function, it actually fits in better with
Swift's conventions to define map in an extension to Array:

```
extension Array {
    func map<T>(transform: Element -> T) -> [T] {
        var result:  [T]  = []
        for x in self {
            result.append(transform(x))
        }
        return result
    }
}
```

The Element type we use in the definition of the function's transform
argument comes from Swift's definition of Array being generic over Element.

Instead of writing map(xs, transform), we can now call Array's map function by
writing xs.map(transform):

```
func genericComputeArray<T>(xs: [Int], transform: Int -> T) -> [T]  {
    return xs.map(transform)
}
```

You'll be glad to hear that you actually don't have to define the map function
yourself this way, because it's already part of Swift's standard library (actually,
it's defined on the SequenceType protocol, but we'll get to that later in the
chapter about generators and sequences). The point of this chapter is *not* to
argue that you should define map yourself; we want to show you that there is
no magic involved in the definition of map — you *could* have easily defined it
yourself!

Top-Level Functions vs. Extensions

You might have noticed that we've used two different styles of declaring
functions in this section: top-level functions, and extensions on the type they
operate on. As long as we were in the process of motivating the map function,
we showed examples as top-level functions for the sake of simplicity. However,
in the end, we've defined the final generic version of map as an extension on
Array, similar to how it's defined in Swift's standard library.

In the standard library's first iteration, top-level functions still were pervasive,
but with Swift 2.0, the language is clearly moving away from this pattern. With

protocol extensions, third-party developers now have a powerful tool for defining their own extensions — not only on specific types like Array, but also on protocols like SequenceType.

We recommend following this convention and defining functions that operate on a certain type as extensions to that type. This has the advantage of better autocompletion, less ambiguous naming, and (often) more clearly structured code.

Filter

The map function is not the only function in Swift's standard array library that uses generics. In the upcoming sections, we will introduce a few others.

Suppose we have an array containing strings, representing the contents of a directory:

```
let exampleFiles = ["README.md", "HelloWorld.swift", "FlappyBird.swift"]
```

Now suppose we want an array of all the .swift files. This is easy to compute with a simple loop:

```
func getSwiftFiles(files: [String]) -> [String] {
    var result: [String] = []
    for file in files {
        if file .hasSuffix(".swift") {
            result.append(file)
        }
    }
    return result
}
```

We can now use this function to ask for the Swift files in our exampleFiles array:

```
getSwiftFiles(exampleFiles)
```

```
["HelloWorld.swift", "FlappyBird.swift"]
```

Of course, we can generalize the getSwiftFiles function. For instance, instead of hardcoding the .swift extension, we could pass an additional String argument to check against. We could then use the same function to check for

.swift or .md files. But what if we want to find all the files without a file extension, or the files starting with the string "Hello"?

To perform such queries, we define a general purpose function called filter. Just as we saw previously with map, the filter function takes a *function* as an argument. This function has the type Element -> Bool — for every element of the array, this function will determine whether or not it should be included in the result:

```
extension Array {
    func filter (includeElement: Element -> Bool) -> [Element] {
        var result: [Element] = []
        for x in self where includeElement(x) {
            result.append(x)
        }
        return result
    }
}
```

It is easy to define getSwiftFiles in terms of filter:

```
func getSwiftFiles2(files: [String]) -> [String] {
    return files . filter { file in file .hasSuffix(".swift") }
}
```

Just like map, the array type already has a filter function defined in Swift's standard library, so there's no need to reimplement it, other than as an exercise.

Now you might wonder: is there an even more general purpose function that can be used to define *both* map and filter? In the last part of this chapter, we will answer that question.

Reduce

Once again, we will consider a few simple functions before defining a generic function that captures a more general pattern.

It is straightforward to define a function that sums all the integers in an array:

```
func sum(xs: [Int]) -> Int {
    var result: Int = 0
```

```
    for x in xs {
        result += x
    }
    return result
}
```

We can use this sum function like so:

```
sum([1, 2, 3, 4])
```

```
10
```

We can also define a product function that computes the product of all the integers in an array using a similar **for** loop as sum:

```
func product(xs: [Int]) -> Int {
    var result: Int = 1
    for x in xs {
        result = x * result
    }
    return result
}
```

Similarly, we may want to concatenate all the strings in an array:

```
func concatenate(xs: [String]) -> String {
    var result: String = ""
    for x in xs {
        result += x
    }
    return result
}
```

Or, we can choose to concatenate all the strings in an array, inserting a separate header line and newline characters after every element:

```
func prettyPrintArray(xs: [String]) -> String {
    var result: String = "Entries in the array xs:\n"
    for x in xs {
        result = "   " + result + x + "\n"
    }
    return result
}
```

What do all these functions have in common? They all initialize a variable, result, with some value. They proceed by iterating over all the elements of the input array, xs, updating the result somehow. To define a generic function that can capture this pattern, there are two pieces of information that we need to abstract over: the initial value assigned to the result variable, and the *function* used to update the result in every iteration.

With this in mind, we arrive at the following definition for the reduce function that captures this pattern:

```
extension Array {
    func reduce<T>(initial: T, combine: (T, Element) -> T) -> T {
        var result = initial
        for x in self {
            result = combine(result, x)
        }
        return result
    }
}
```

This function is generic in two ways: for any *input array* of type [Element], it will compute a result of type T. To do this, it needs an initial value of type T (to assign to the result variable), and a function, combine: (T, Element) -> T, which is used to update the result variable in the body of the **for** loop. In some functional languages, such as OCaml and Haskell, reduce functions are called fold or fold_left.

We can define every function we have seen in this chapter thus far using reduce. Here are a few examples:

```
func sumUsingReduce(xs: [Int]) -> Int {
    return xs.reduce(0) { result, x in result + x }
}
```

Instead of writing a closure, we could have also written just the operator as the last argument. This makes the code even shorter, as illustrated by the following two functions:

```
func productUsingReduce(xs: [Int]) -> Int {
    return xs.reduce(1, combine: *)
}

func concatUsingReduce(xs: [String]) -> String {
    return xs.reduce("", combine: +)
```

}

Once again, defining reduce ourselves is just an exercise. Swift's standard library already provides the reduce function for arrays.

We can use reduce to define new generic functions. For example, suppose that we have an array of arrays that we want to flatten into a single array. We could write a function that uses a **for** loop:

```
func flatten<T>(xss: [[T]]) -> [T] {
    var result: [T] = []
    for xs in xss {
        result += xs
    }
    return result
}
```

Using reduce, however, we can write this function as follows:

```
func flattenUsingReduce<T>(xss: [[T]]) -> [T] {
    return xss.reduce([]) { result, xs in result + xs }
}
```

In fact, we can even redefine map and filter using reduce:

```
extension Array {
    func mapUsingReduce<T>(transform: Element -> T) -> [T] {
        return reduce([]) { result, x in
            return result + [transform(x)]
        }
    }

    func filterUsingReduce(includeElement: Element -> Bool) -> [Element] {
        return reduce([]) { result, x in
            return includeElement(x) ? result + [x] : result
        }
    }
}
```

The fact that we're able to express all these other functions using reduce shows how reduce captures a very common programming pattern in a generic way: iterating over an array to compute a result.

Please note: while defining everything in terms of reduce is an interesting exercise, in practice it's often a bad idea. The reason for this is that your code will currently end up making lots of copies of the resulting array during runtime, i.e. it has to allocate, deallocate, and copy the contents of a lot of memory. Defining map, for example, using a mutable result array as we did before is vastly more efficient. In theory, the compiler could optimize this code to be as fast as the version with the mutable result array, but Swift 2.0 doesn't do this. For more details, check out our Advanced Swift[1] book.

Putting It All Together

To conclude this section, we will give a small example of map, filter , and reduce in action.

Suppose we have the following **struct** definition, consisting of a city's name and population (measured in thousands of inhabitants):

```
struct City {
    let name: String
    let population: Int
}
```

We can define several example cities:

```
let paris = City(name: "Paris", population: 2241)
let madrid = City(name: "Madrid", population: 3165)
let amsterdam = City(name: "Amsterdam", population: 827)
let berlin = City(name: "Berlin", population: 3562)

let cities = [paris, madrid, amsterdam, berlin]
```

Now suppose we would like to print a list of cities with at least one million inhabitants, together with their total populations. We can define a helper function that scales up the inhabitants:

```
extension City {
    func cityByScalingPopulation() -> City {
        return City(name: name, population: population * 1000)
    }
}
```

1 https://objc.io/books/advanced-swift

Now we can use all the ingredients we have seen in this chapter to write the following statement:

```
cities . filter  {  $0.population > 1000 }
    .map { $0.cityByScalingPopulation() }
    .reduce("City: Population") { result, c in
        return result + "\n" + "\(c.name): \(c.population)"
    }
```

```
City:  Population
Paris:  2241000
Madrid: 3165000
Berlin: 3562000
```

We start by filtering out those cities that have less than one million inhabitants. We then map our cityByScalingPopulation function over the remaining cities. Finally, using the reduce function, we compute a String with a list of city names and populations. Here we use the map, filter , and reduce definitions from the Array type in Swift's standard library. As a result, we can chain together the results of our maps and filters nicely. The cities . filter (..) expression computes an array, on which we call map; we call reduce on the result of this call to obtain our final result.

Generics vs. the Any Type

Aside from generics, Swift also supports an Any type that can represent values of any type. On the surface, this may seem similar to generics. Both the Any type and generics can be used to define functions accepting different types of arguments. However, it is very important to understand the difference: generics can be used to define flexible functions, the types of which are still checked by the compiler; the Any type can be used to dodge Swift's type system (and should be avoided whenever possible).

Let's consider the simplest possible example, which is a function that does nothing but return its argument. Using generics, we might write the following:

```
func noOp<T>(x: T) -> T {
    return x
}
```

Using the Any type, we might write the following:

```
func noOpAny(x: Any) -> Any {
    return x
}
```

Both noOp and noOpAny will accept any argument. The crucial difference is what we know about the value being returned. In the definition of noOp, we can clearly see that the return value is the same as the input value. This is not the case for noOpAny, which may return a value of any type — even a type different from the original input. We might also give the following, erroneous definition of noOpAny:

```
func noOpAnyWrong(x: Any) -> Any {
    return 0
}
```

Using the Any type evades Swift's type system. However, trying to return 0 in the body of the noOp function defined using generics will cause a type error. Furthermore, any function that calls noOpAny does not know to which type the result must be cast. There are all kinds of possible runtime exceptions that may be raised as a result.

Finally, the *type* of a generic function is extremely informative. Consider the following generic version of the function composition operator, >>>, that we defined in the chapter Wrapping Core Image:

```
infix operator >>> { associativity left }
func >>> <A, B, C>(f: A -> B, g: B -> C) -> A -> C {
    return { x in g(f(x)) }
}
```

The type of this function is so generic that it completely determines how the *function itself* is defined. We'll try to give an informal argument for this here.

We need to produce a value of type C. As there is nothing else we know about C, there is no value that we can return immediately. If we knew that C was some concrete type, like Int or Bool, we could potentially return a value of that type, such as 5 or True, respectively. As our function must work *for any* type C, we cannot do so. The only argument to the >>> operator that refers to C is the function g: B -> C. Therefore, the only way to get our hands on a value of type C is by applying the function g to a value of type B.

Similarly, the only way to produce a B is by applying f to a value of type A. The only value of type A that we have is the final argument to our operator.

Therefore, this definition of function composition is the only possible function that has this generic type.

In the same way, we can define a generic function that curries any function expecting a tuple of two arguments, thereby producing the corresponding curried version:

```
func curry<A, B, C>(f: (A, B) -> C) -> A -> B -> C {
    return { x in { y in f(x, y) } }
}
```

We no longer need to define two different versions of the same function, the curried and the uncurried, as we did in the last chapter. Instead, generic functions such as curry can be used to transform *functions* — computing the curried version from the uncurried. Once again, the type of this function is so generic that it (almost) gives a complete specification: there really is only one sensible implementation.

Using generics allows you to write flexible functions without compromising type safety; if you use the Any type, you're pretty much on your own.

Notes

The history of generics traces back to Strachey (2000), Girard's *System F* (1972), and Reynolds (1974). Note that these authors refer to generics as (parametric) polymorphism, a term that is still used in many other functional languages. Many object-oriented languages use the term polymorphism to refer to implicit casts arising from subtyping, so the term generics was introduced to disambiguate between the two concepts.

The process that we sketched informally above, motivating why there can only be one possible function with the generic type

```
(f: A -> B, g: B -> C) -> A -> C
```

can be made mathematically precise. This was first done by Reynolds (1983); later Wadler (1989) referred to this as *Theorems for free!* — emphasizing how you can compute a theorem about a generic function from its type.

Optionals

5

Swift's *optional types* can be used to represent values that may be missing or computations that may fail. This chapter describes how to work with optional types effectively, and how they fit well within the functional programming paradigm.

Case Study: Dictionaries

In addition to arrays, Swift has special support for working with *dictionaries*. A dictionary is a collection of key-value pairs, and it provides an efficient way to find the value associated with a certain key. The syntax for creating dictionaries is similar to arrays:

```
let cities = ["Paris": 2241, "Madrid": 3165, "Amsterdam": 827, "Berlin": 3562]
```

This dictionary stores the population of several European cities. In this example, the key "Paris" is associated with the value 2241; that is, Paris has about 2,241,000 inhabitants.

As with arrays, the Dictionary type is generic. The type of dictionaries takes two type parameters, corresponding to the types of the stored keys and stored values, respectively. In our example, the city dictionary has type Dictionary<String, Int>. There is also a shorthand notation, [String: Int].

We can look up the value associated with a key using the same notation as array indexing:

```
let madridPopulation: Int = cities["Madrid"]
```

This example, however, does not type check. The problem is that the key "Madrid" may not be in the cities dictionary — and what value should be returned if it is not? We cannot guarantee that the dictionary lookup operation *always* returns an Int for every key. Swift's *optional* types track the possibility of this kind of failure. The correct way to write the example above would be the following:

```
let madridPopulation: Int? = cities["Madrid"]
```

Instead of having type Int, the madridPopulation example has the optional type Int?. A value of type Int? is either an Int or a special 'missing' value, **nil**.

We can check whether or not the lookup was successful:

```
if madridPopulation != nil {
    print("The population of Madrid is \(madridPopulation! * 1000)")
} else {
    print("Unknown city: Madrid")
}
```

If madridPopulation is not **nil**, then the branch is executed. To refer to the underlying Int, we write madridPopulation!. The post-fix ! operator forces an optional to a non-optional type. To compute the total population of Madrid, we force the optional madridPopulation to an Int, and multiply it by 1000.

Swift has a special *optional binding* mechanism that lets you avoid writing the ! suffix. We can combine the definition of madridPopulation and the check above into a single statement:

```
if let madridPopulation = cities["Madrid"] {
    print("The population of Madrid is \(madridPopulation * 1000)")
} else {
    print("Unknown city: Madrid")
}
```

If the lookup, cities["Madrid"], is successful, we can use the variable madridPopulation of type Int in the then-branch. Note that we no longer need to explicitly use the forced unwrapping operator.

Given the choice, we'd recommend using optional binding over forced unwrapping. Forced unwrapping may crash if you have a **nil** value; optional binding encourages you to handle exceptional cases explicitly, thereby avoiding runtime errors. Unchecked usage of the forced unwrapping of optional types or Swift's implicitly unwrapped optionals can be a bad code smell, indicating the possibility of runtime errors.

Swift also provides a safer alternative to the ! operator, which requires an additional default value to return when applied to **nil**. Roughly speaking, it can be defined as follows:

```
infix operator ??

func ??<T>(optional: T?, defaultValue: T) -> T {
    if let x = optional {
        return x
    } else {
        return defaultValue
    }
```

}

The ?? operator checks whether or not its optional argument is **nil**. If it is, it returns its defaultValue argument; otherwise, it returns the optional's underlying value.

There is one problem with this definition: the defaultValue will be evaluated, regardless of whether or not the optional is **nil**. This is usually undesirable behavior: an if-then-else statement should only execute *one* of its branches, depending on whether or not the associated condition is true. Similarly, the ?? operator should only evaluate the defaultValue argument when the optional argument is **nil**. As an illustration, suppose we were to call ??, as follows:

optional ?? defaultValue

In this example, we really do not want to evaluate defaultValue if the **optional** variable is non-nil — it could be a very expensive computation that we only want to run if it is absolutely necessary. We can resolve this issue as follows:

```
func ??<T>(optional: T?, defaultValue: () -> T) -> T {
    if let x = optional {
        return x
    } else {
        return defaultValue()
    }
}
```

Instead of providing a default value of type T, we now provide one of type () -> T. The code in the defaultValue closure is now only executed when we pass it its (void) argument. In this definition, this code is only executed in the else branch, as we intended. The only drawback is that when calling the ?? operator, we need to create an explicit closure for the default value. For example, we would need to write the following:

myOptional ?? { myDefaultValue }

The definition in the Swift standard library avoids the need for creating explicit closures by using Swift's autoclosure type attribute. This implicitly wraps any arguments to the ?? operator in the required closure. As a result, we can provide the same interface that we initially had, but without requiring the user to create an explicit closure wrapping the defaultValue argument. The actual definition used in Swift's standard library is as follows:

```
infix operator ?? { associativity right precedence 110 }

func ??<T>(optional: T?, @autoclosure defaultValue: () -> T) -> T {
    if let x = optional {
        return x
    } else {
        return defaultValue()
    }
}
```

The ?? operator provides a safer alternative to the forced optional unwrapping without being as verbose as the optional binding.

Working with Optionals

Swift's optional values make the possibility of failure explicit. This can be cumbersome, especially when combining multiple optional results. There are several techniques to facilitate the use of optionals.

Optional Chaining

First of all, Swift has a special mechanism, *optional chaining*, for selecting methods or attributes in nested classes or structs. Consider the following (fragment of a) model for processing customer orders:

```
struct Order {
    let orderNumber: Int
    let person: Person?
}

struct Person {
    let name: String
    let address: Address?
}

struct Address {
    let streetName: String
    let city: String
    let state: String?
}
```

Given an Order, how can we find the state of the customer? We could use the explicit unwrapping operator:

```
order.person!.address!.state!
```

Doing so, however, may cause runtime exceptions if any of the intermediate data is missing. It would be much safer to use optional binding:

```
if let myPerson = order.person {
    if let myAddress = myPerson.address {
        if let myState = myAddress.state {
            // ...
```

But this is rather verbose. Using optional chaining, this example would become:

```
if let myState = order.person?.address?.state {
    print("This order will be shipped to \(myState)")
} else {
    print("Unknown person, address, or state.")
}
```

Instead of forcing the unwrapping of intermediate types, we use the question mark operator to try and unwrap the optional types. When any of the component selections fails, the whole chain of selection statements returns **nil**.

Branching on Optionals

We've already discussed the **if let** optional binding mechanism above, but Swift has two other branch statements, **switch** and **guard**, that are especially suited to work with optionals.

To match an optional value in a **switch** statement, we simply add the ? suffix to every pattern in a **case** branch. If we're not interested in a specific value, we can also match against Optional's None or Some values directly:

```
switch madridPopulation {
    case 0?: print("Nobody in Madrid")
    case (1..<1000)?: print("Less than a million in Madrid")
    case .Some(let x): print("\(x) people in Madrid")
    case .None: print("We don't know about Madrid")
}
```

The **guard** statement is designed to exit the current scope early if some condition is not met. A very common use case is to combine it with optional binding to handle the None case when no value is present. This makes it very clear that any code following the **guard** statement requires the value to be present and will not be executed if it isn't. For example, we could rewrite the code to print out the number of inhabitants of a given city like this:

```
func populationDescriptionForCity(city: String) -> String? {
    guard let population = cities[city] else { return nil }
    return "The population of Madrid is \(population * 1000)"
}

populationDescriptionForCity("Madrid")

The population of Madrid is 3165000
The population of Madrid is
3165000
3165 people in Madrid
Optional("The population of Madrid is
3165000")
```

After the **guard** statement, we have the non-optional population value to work with. Using **guard** statements in this fashion makes the control flow simpler than nesting **if let** statements.

Optional Mapping

The ? operator lets us select methods or fields of optional values. However, there are plenty of other examples where you may want to manipulate an optional value, if it exists, and return **nil** otherwise. Consider the following example:

```
func incrementOptional(optional: Int?) -> Int? {
    guard let x = optional else { return nil }
    return x + 1
}
```

The incrementOptional example behaves similarly to the ? operator: if the optional value is **nil**, the result is **nil**; otherwise, some computation is performed.

We can generalize both incrementOptional and the ? operator and define a map function on optionals. Rather than only increment a value of type Int?, as we did in incrementOptional, we pass the operation we wish to perform as an argument to the map function:

```
extension Optional {
    func map<U>(transform: Wrapped -> U) -> U? {
        guard let x = self else { return nil }
        return transform(x)
    }
}
```

This map function takes a transform function of type Wrapped -> U as argument. If the optional value is not **nil**, it applies transform to it and returns the result; otherwise, the map function returns **nil**. This map function is part of the Swift standard library.

Using map, we write the incrementOptional function as the following:

```
func incrementOptional2(optional: Int?) -> Int? {
    return optional.map { $0 + 1 }
}
```

Of course, we can also use map to project fields or methods from optional structs and classes, similar to the ? operator.

Why is this function called map? What does it have in common with array computations? There is a good reason for calling both of these functions map, but we will defer this discussion for the moment and return to it in the chapter about functors, applicative functors, and monads.

Optional Binding Revisited

The map function shows one way to manipulate optional values, but many others exist. Consider the following example:

```
let x: Int? = 3
let y: Int? = nil
let z: Int? = x + y
```

This program is not accepted by the Swift compiler. Can you spot the error?

The problem is that addition only works on Int values, rather than the optional Int? values we have here. To resolve this, we could introduce nested **if** statements, as follows:

```
func addOptionals(optionalX: Int?, optionalY: Int?) -> Int? {
    if let x = optionalX {
        if let y = optionalY {
            return x + y
        }
    }
    return nil
}
```

However, instead of the deep nesting, we can also bind multiple optionals at the same time:

```
func addOptionals(optionalX: Int?, optionalY: Int?) -> Int? {
    if let x = optionalX, y = optionalY {
        return x + y
    }
    return nil
}
```

Even shorter, we can also use a **guard** statement to exit early in case of missing values:

```
func addOptionals(optionalX: Int?, optionalY: Int?) -> Int? {
    guard let x = optionalX, y = optionalY else { return nil }
    return x + y
}
```

This may seem like a contrived example, but manipulating optional values can happen all the time. Suppose we have the following dictionary, associating countries with their capital cities:

```
let capitals = [
    "France": "Paris",
    "Spain": "Madrid",
    "The Netherlands": "Amsterdam",
    "Belgium": "Brussels"
]
```

In order to write a function that returns the number of inhabitants for the capital of a given country, we use the capitals dictionary in conjunction with the cities dictionary defined previously. For each dictionary lookup, we have to make sure that it actually returned a result:

```
func populationOfCapital(country: String) -> Int? {
```

```
    guard let capital = capitals[country], population = cities[capital]
        else { return nil }
    return population * 1000
}
```

Both optional chaining and **if let** (or **guard let**) are special constructs in the language to make working with optionals easier. However, Swift offers yet another way to solve the problem above: the function flatMap in the standard library. The flatMap function is defined on multiple types, and in the case of optionals, it looks like this:

```
extension Optional {
    func flatMap<U>(f: Wrapped -> U?) -> U? {
        guard let x = self else { return nil }
        return f(x)
    }
}
```

The flatMap function checks whether an optional value is non-**nil**. If it is, we pass it on to the argument function f; if the optional argument is **nil**, the result is also **nil**.

Using this function, we can now write our examples as follows:

```
func addOptionals2(optionalX: Int?, optionalY: Int?) -> Int? {
    return optionalX.flatMap { x in
        optionalY.flatMap { y in
            return x + y
        }
    }
}
```

```
func populationOfCapital2(country: String) -> Int? {
    return capitals[country].flatMap { capital in
        cities [capital].flatMap { population in
            return population * 1000
        }
    }
}
```

Instead of nesting the flatMap calls, we can also rewrite populationOfCapital2 in such a way that the calls are chained, thereby making the structure of the code more shallow:

```
func populationOfCapital3(country: String) -> Int? {
    return capitals[country].flatMap { capital in
        return cities [capital]
    }. flatMap { population in
        return population * 1000
    }
}
```

We do not want to advocate that flatMap is the 'right' way to combine optional values. Instead, we hope to show that optional binding is not magically built-in to the Swift compiler, but rather a control structure you can implement yourself using a higher-order function.

Why Optionals?

What's the point of introducing an explicit optional type? For programmers used to Objective-C, working with optional types may seem strange at first. The Swift type system is rather rigid: whenever we have an optional type, we have to deal with the possibility of it being **nil**. We have had to write new functions like map to manipulate optional values. In Objective-C, you have more flexibility. For instance, when translating the example above to Objective-C, there is no compiler error:

```
- (int)populationOfCapital:(NSString *)country
{
    return [self. cities [self.capitals[country]] intValue] * 1000;
}
```

We can pass in **nil** for the name of a country, and we get back a result of 0. Everything is fine. In many languages without optionals, null pointers are a source of danger. Much less so in Objective-C. In Objective-C, you can safely send messages to **nil**, and depending on the return type, you either get **nil**, 0, or similar "zero-like" values. Why change this behavior in Swift?

The choice for an explicit optional type fits with the increased static safety of Swift. A strong type system catches errors before code is executed, and an explicit optional type helps protect you from unexpected crashes arising from missing values.

The default zero-like behavior employed by Objective-C has its drawbacks. You may want to distinguish between failure (a key is not in the dictionary) and success-returning **nil** (a key is in the dictionary, but associated with **nil**). To do that in Objective-C, you have to use NSNull.

While it is safe in Objective-C to send messages to **nil**, it is often not safe to use them.

Let's say we want to create an attributed string. If we pass in **nil** as the argument for country, the capital will also be **nil**, but NSAttributedString will crash when trying to initialize it with a **nil** value:

```
- (NSAttributedString *)attributedCapital:(NSString *)country
{
    NSString *capital = self.capitals[country];
    NSDictionary *attr = @{ /* ... */ };
    return [[NSAttributedString alloc] initWithString:capital attributes:attr];
}
```

While crashes like the above don't happen too often, almost every developer has had code like this crash. Most of the time, these crashes are detected during debugging, but it is very possible to ship code without noticing that, in some cases, a variable might unexpectedly be **nil**. Therefore, many programmers use asserts to explicitly document this behavior. For example, we can add an NSParameterAssert to make sure we crash quickly when the country is **nil**:

```
- (NSAttributedString *)attributedCapital:(NSString *)country
{
    NSParameterAssert(country);
    NSString *capital = self.capitals[country];
    NSDictionary *attr = @{ /* ... */ };
    return [[NSAttributedString alloc] initWithString:capital attributes:attr];
}
```

But what if we pass in a country value that doesn't have a matching key in **self**.capitals? This is much more likely, especially when country comes from user input. In such a case, capital will be **nil** and our code will still crash. Of course, this can be fixed easily enough. The point is, however, that it is easier to write *robust* code using **nil** in Swift than in Objective-C.

Finally, using these assertions is inherently non-modular. Suppose we implement a checkCountry method that checks that a non-empty NSString * is supported. We can incorporate this check easily enough:

```
- (NSAttributedString *)attributedCapital:(NSString*)country
{
    NSParameterAssert(country);
    if (checkCountry(country)) {
        // ...
    }
}
```

Now the question arises: should the checkCountry function also assert that its argument is non-**nil**? On one hand, it should not — we have just performed the check in the attributedCapital method. On the other hand, if the checkCountry function only works on non-**nil** values, we should duplicate the assertion. We are forced to choose between exposing an unsafe interface or duplicating assertions. It is also possible to add a nonnull attribute to the signature, which will emit a warning when the method is called with a value that could be **nil**, but this is not common practice in most Objective-C codebases.

In Swift, things are better: function signatures using optionals explicitly state which values may be **nil**. This is invaluable information when working with other people's code. A signature like the following provides a lot of information:

func attributedCapital(country: String) -> NSAttributedString?

Not only are we warned about the possibility of failure, but we know that we must pass a String as argument — and not a **nil** value. A crash like the one we described above will not happen. Furthermore, this is information *checked* by the compiler. Documentation goes out of date easily; you can always trust function signatures.

When dealing with scalar values, optionality is even more tricky in Objective-C. Consider the following sample, which tries to find mentions of a specific keyword in a string:

```
NSString *someString = ...;
if ([someString rangeOfString:@"swift"].location != NSNotFound) {
    NSLog(@"Someone mentioned swift!");
}
```

It looks innocent enough: if rangeOfString: does not find the string, then the location will be set to NSNotFound. NSNotFound is defined as NSIntegerMax. This code is almost correct, and the problem is hard to see at first sight: when someString is **nil**, then rangeOfString: will return a structure filled with zeroes, and the location will return 0. The check will then succeed, and the code inside the if-statement will be executed.

With optionals, this can not happen. If we wanted to port this code to Swift, we would need to make some structural changes. The above code would be rejected by the compiler, and the type system would not allow you to run rangeOfString: on a **nil** value. Instead, you first need to unwrap it:

```swift
if let someString = ... {
    if someString.rangeOfString("swift").location != NSNotFound {
        print("Found")
    }
}
```

The type system will help in catching subtle errors for you. Some of these errors would have been easily detected during development, but others might accidentally end up in production code. By using optionals consistently, this class of errors can be eliminated automatically.

Case Study: QuickCheck

6

In recent years, testing has become much more prevalent in Objective-C. Many popular libraries are now tested automatically with continuous integration tools. The standard framework for writing unit tests is XCTest. Additionally, a lot of third-party frameworks (such as Specta, Kiwi, and FBSnapshotTestCase) are already available, and a number of new frameworks are currently being developed in Swift.

All of these frameworks follow a similar pattern: tests typically consist of some fragment of code, together with an expected result. The code is then executed, and its result is compared to the expected result defined in the test. Different libraries test at different levels — some test individual methods, some test classes, and some perform integration testing (running the entire app). In this chapter, we will build a small library for property-based testing of Swift functions. We will build this library in an iterative fashion, improving it step by step.

When writing unit tests, the input data is static and defined by the programmer. For example, when unit testing an addition method, we might write a test that verifies that 1 + 1 is equal to 2. If the implementation of addition changes in such a way that this property is broken, the test will fail. More generally, however, we could choose to test that the addition is commutative — in other words, that a + b is equal to b + a. To test this, we could write a test case that verifies that 42 + 7 is equal to 7 + 42.

QuickCheck (Claessen and Hughes 2000) is a Haskell library for random testing. Instead of writing individual unit tests, each of which tests that a function is correct for some particular input, QuickCheck allows you to describe abstract *properties* of your functions and *generate* tests to verify these properties. When a property passes, it doesn't necessarily prove that the property is correct. Rather, QuickCheck aims to find boundary conditions that invalidate the property. In this chapter, we'll build a (partial) Swift port of QuickCheck.

This is best illustrated with an example. Suppose we want to verify that addition is a commutative operation. To do so, we start by writing a function that checks whether x + y is equal to y + x for the two integers x and y:

```swift
func plusIsCommutative(x: Int, y: Int) -> Bool {
    return x + y == y + x
}
```

Checking this statement with QuickCheck is as simple as calling the check function:

```
check("Plus should be commutative", plusIsCommutative)
```

```
"Plus should be commutative" passed 10 tests.
()
```

The check function works by calling the plusIsCommutative function with two random integers, over and over again. If the statement isn't true, it will print out the input that caused the test to fail. The key insight here is that we can describe abstract *properties* of our code (like commutativity) using *functions* that return a Bool (like plusIsCommutative). The check function now uses this property to *generate* unit tests, giving much better code coverage than you could achieve using handwritten unit tests.

Of course, not all tests pass. For example, we can define a statement that describes that subtraction is commutative:

```
func minusIsCommutative(x: Int, y: Int) -> Bool {
    return x - y == y - x
}
```

Now, if we run QuickCheck on this function, we will get a failing test case:

```
check("Minus should be commutative", minusIsCommutative)
```

```
"Minus should be commutative" doesn't hold: (0, 1)
()
```

Using Swift's syntax for trailing closures, we can also write tests directly, without defining the property (such as plusIsCommutative or minusIsCommutative) separately:

```
check("Additive identity") { (x: Int) in x + 0 == x }
```

```
"Additive identity" passed 10 tests.
()
```

Of course, there are many other similar properties of standard arithmetic that we can test. We will cover more interesting tests and properties shortly. Before we do so, however, we will give some more details about how QuickCheck is implemented.

Building QuickCheck

In order to build our Swift implementation of QuickCheck, we will need to do a couple of things.

→ First, we need a way to generate random values for different types.

→ Using these random value generators, we need to implement the check function, which passes random values to its argument property.

→ If a test fails, we would like to make the test input as small as possible. For example, if our test fails on an array with 100 elements, we'll try to make it smaller and see if the test still fails.

→ Finally, we'll need to do some extra work to make sure our check function works on types that have generics.

Generating Random Values

First, let's define a protocol that knows how to generate arbitrary values. This protocol contains only one function, arbitrary, which returns a value of type **Self**, i.e. an instance of the class or struct that implements the Arbitrary protocol:

```
protocol Arbitrary {
    static func arbitrary() -> Self
}
```

So let's write an instance for Int. We use the arc4random function from the standard library and convert it into an Int. Note that this only generates positive integers. A real implementation of the library would generate negative integers as well, but we'll try to keep things simple in this chapter:

```
extension Int: Arbitrary {
    static func arbitrary() -> Int {
        return Int(arc4random())
    }
}
```

Now we can generate random integers, like this:

```
Int.arbitrary()
```

To generate random strings, we need to do a little bit more work. We start off by generating random characters:

```
extension Character: Arbitrary {
    static func arbitrary() -> Character {
        return Character(UnicodeScalar(Int.random(from: 65, to: 90)))
    }
}
```

Then, we generate a random length between 0 and 40 — x — using the random function defined below. Then, we generate x random characters, and reduce them into a string. Note that we currently only generate capital letters as random characters. In a production library, we should generate longer strings that contain arbitrary characters:

```
func tabulate<A>(times: Int, transform: Int -> A) -> [A] {
    return (0..<times).map(transform)
}

extension Int {
    static func random(from from: Int, to: Int) -> Int {
        return from + (Int(arc4random()) % (to - from))
    }
}

extension String: Arbitrary {
    static func arbitrary() -> String {
        let randomLength = Int.random(from: 0, to: 40)
        let randomCharacters = tabulate(randomLength) { _ in
            Character.arbitrary()
        }
        return String(randomCharacters)
    }
}
```

We use the tabulate function to fill an array with the numbers from 0 to times-1. By using the map function, we then generate an array with the values f(0), f(1), ..., f(times-1). The arbitrary extension to String uses the tabulate function to populate an array of random characters.

We can call it in the same way as we generate random Ints, except that we call it on the String class:

String.arbitrary ()

WTGYFDTDCMQCLSKPJULMLHTVVMEUVWMMG

Implementing the check Function

Now we are ready to implement a first version of our check function. The
check1 function consists of a simple loop that generates random input for the
argument property in every iteration. If a counterexample is found, it is
printed, and the function returns; if no counterexample is found, the check1
function reports the number of successful tests that have passed. (Note that
we called the function check1, because we'll write the final version a bit later.)

```
func check1<A: Arbitrary>(message: String, _ property: A -> Bool) -> () {
    for _ in 0..<numberOfIterations {
        let value = A.arbitrary ()
        guard property(value) else {
            print("\"\(message)\" doesn't hold: \(value)")
            return
        }
    }
    print("\"\(message)\" passed \(numberOfIterations) tests.")
}
```

We could have chosen to use a more functional style by writing this function
using reduce or map, rather than a **for** loop. In this example, however, **for** loops
make perfect sense: we want to iterate an operation a fixed number of times,
stopping execution once a counterexample has been found — and **for** loops are
perfect for that.

Here's how we can use this function to test properties:

```
extension CGSize {
    var area: CGFloat {
        return width * height
    }
}

extension CGSize: Arbitrary {
    static func arbitrary() -> CGSize {
        return CGSize(width: CGFloat.arbitrary(),
            height: CGFloat.arbitrary())
    }
```

```
}
```

```
check1("Area should be at least 0") { (size: CGSize) in size.area >= 0 }
```

```
"Area should be at least 0" doesn't hold: (-675.342363695461,
543.87011228685)
()
```

Here we can see a good example of when QuickCheck can be very useful: it finds an edge case for us. If a size has exactly one negative component, our area function will return a negative number. When used as part of a CGRect, a CGSize can have negative values. When writing ordinary unit tests, it is easy to oversee this case, because sizes usually only have positive components.

Making Values Smaller

If we run our check1 function on strings, we might receive a rather long failure message:

```
check1("Every string starts with Hello") { (s: String) in
    s.hasPrefix("Hello")
}
```

```
"Every string starts with Hello" doesn't hold:
PMRVWLLVLBRJXMTUFUBCDBVBBE
()
```

Ideally, we'd like our failing input to be as short as possible. In general, the smaller the counterexample, the easier it is to spot which piece of code is causing the failure. In this example, the counterexample is still pretty easy to understand, but this may not always be the case. Imagine a complicated condition on arrays or dictionaries that fails for some unclear reason — diagnosing why a test is failing is much easier with a minimal counterexample. In principle, the user could try to trim the input that triggered the failure and attempt rerunning the test — rather than place the burden on the user — however, we will automate this process.

To do so, we will make an extra protocol called Smaller, which does only one thing — it tries to shrink the counterexample:

```
protocol Smaller {
    func smaller() -> Self?
```

```
}
```

are cases when it is not clear how to shrink test data any further. For example, there is no way to shrink an empty array. We will return **nil** in that case.

In our instance, for integers, we just try to divide the integer by two until we reach zero:

```
extension Int: Smaller {
    func smaller() -> Int? {
        return self == 0 ? nil : self / 2
    }
}
```

We can now test our instance:

```
100.smaller()
```

```
Optional(50)
```

For strings, we just drop the first character (unless the string is empty):

```
extension String: Smaller {
    func smaller() -> String? {
        return isEmpty ? nil : String(characters.dropFirst())
    }
}
```

To use the Smaller protocol in the check function, we will need the ability to shrink any test data generated by our check function. To do so, we will redefine our Arbitrary protocol to extend the Smaller protocol:

```
protocol Arbitrary: Smaller {
    static func arbitrary() -> Self
}
```

Repeatedly Shrinking

We can now redefine our check function to shrink any test data that triggers a failure. To do this, we use the iterateWhile function, which takes a condition and an initial value, and repeatedly applies a function as long as the condition holds:

```
func iterateWhile<A>(condition: A -> Bool, initial : A, next: A -> A?) -> A {
    if let x = next( initial ) where condition(x) {
        return iterateWhile(condition, initial : x, next: next)
    }
    return initial
}
```

Using iterateWhile, we can now repeatedly shrink counterexamples that we uncover during testing:

```
func check2<A: Arbitrary>(message: String, _ property: A -> Bool) -> () {
    for _ in 0..<numberOfIterations {
        let value = A.arbitrary ()
        guard property(value) else {
            let smallerValue = iterateWhile({ !property($0) }, initial : value) {
                $0.smaller()
            }
            print("\"\(message)\" doesn't hold: \(smallerValue)")
            return
        }
    }
    print("\"\(message)\" passed \(numberOfIterations) tests.")
}
```

This function is doing quite a bit: generating random input values, checking whether they satisfy the property argument, and repeatedly shrinking a counterexample, once one is found. One advantage of defining the repeated shrinking using iterateWhile, rather than a separate while loop, is that the control flow of this piece of code stays reasonably simple.

Arbitrary Arrays

Currently, our check2 function only supports Int and String values. While we are free to define new extensions for other types, such as Bool, things get more complicated when we want to generate arbitrary arrays. As a motivating example, let's write a functional version of QuickSort:

```
func qsort(var array: [Int]) -> [Int] {
    if array.isEmpty { return [] }
    let pivot = array.removeAtIndex(0)
    let lesser = array. filter { $0 < pivot }
    let greater = array. filter { $0 >= pivot }
    return qsort(lesser) + [pivot] + qsort(greater)
}
```

```
}
```

We can also try to write a property to check our version of QuickSort against the built-in sort function:

```
check2("qsort should behave like sort") { (x: [Int]) in
    return qsort(x) == x.sort(<)
}
```

However, the compiler warns us that [Int] doesn't conform to the Arbitrary protocol. Before we can implement Arbitrary, we first have to implement Smaller. As a first step, we provide a simple definition that drops the first element in the array:

```
extension Array: Smaller {
    func smaller() -> [Element]? {
        guard !isEmpty else { return nil }
        return Array(dropFirst())
    }
}
```

We can also write a function that generates an array of arbitrary length for any type that conforms to the Arbitrary protocol:

```
extension Array where Element: Arbitrary {
    static func arbitrary() -> [Element] {
        let randomLength = Int(arc4random() % 50)
        return tabulate(randomLength) { _ in Element.arbitrary() }
    }
}
```

Now what we'd like to do is make Array itself conform to the Arbitrary protocol. However, only arrays with elements that conform to Arbitrary as well can themselves conform to Arbitrary. For example, in order to generate an array of random numbers, we first need to make sure that we can generate random numbers. Ideally, we would write something like this, saying that the elements of an array should also conform to the arbitrary protocol:

```
extension Array: Arbitrary where Element: Arbitrary {
    static func arbitrary() -> [Element] {
        // ...
    }
}
```

Unfortunately, it is currently not possible to express this restriction as a type constraint, making it impossible to write an extension that makes Array conform to the Arbitrary protocol. Instead, we will modify the check2 function.

The problem with the check2<A> function was that it required the type A to be Arbitrary. We will drop this requirement, and instead require the necessary functions, smaller and arbitrary, to be passed in as arguments.

We start by defining an auxiliary struct that contains the two functions we need:

```
struct ArbitraryInstance<T> {
    let arbitrary:  () -> T
    let smaller: T -> T?
}
```

We can now write a helper function that takes an ArbitraryInstance struct as an argument. The definition of checkHelper closely follows the check2 function we saw previously. The only difference between the two is where the arbitrary and smaller functions are defined. In check2, these were constraints on the generic type, <A: Arbitrary>; in checkHelper, they are passed explicitly in the ArbitraryInstance struct:

```
func checkHelper<A>(arbitraryInstance: ArbitraryInstance<A>,
    _ property: A -> Bool, _ message: String) -> ()
{
    for _ in 0..<numberOfIterations {
        let value = arbitraryInstance.arbitrary()
        guard property(value) else {
            let smallerValue = iterateWhile({ !property($0) },
                initial : value, next: arbitraryInstance.smaller)
            print("\"\(message)\" doesn't hold: \(smallerValue)")
            return
        }
    }
    print("\"\(message)\" passed \(numberOfIterations) tests.")
}
```

This is a standard technique: instead of working with functions defined in a protocol, we explicitly pass the required information as an argument. By doing so, we have a bit more flexibility. We no longer rely on Swift to *infer* the required information, but instead have complete control over this ourselves.

We can redefine our check2 function to use the checkHelper function. If we know that we have the desired Arbitrary definitions, we can wrap them in the ArbitraryInstance struct and call checkHelper:

```
func check<X: Arbitrary>(message: String, property: X -> Bool) -> () {
    let instance = ArbitraryInstance(arbitrary: X.arbitrary,
        smaller: { $0.smaller() })
    checkHelper(instance, property, message)
}
```

If we have a type for which we cannot define the desired Arbitrary instance, as is the case with arrays, we can overload the check function and construct the desired ArbitraryInstance struct ourselves:

```
func check<X: Arbitrary>(message: String, _ property: [X] -> Bool) -> () {
    let instance = ArbitraryInstance(arbitrary: Array.arbitrary,
        smaller: { (x: [X]) in x.smaller() })
    checkHelper(instance, property, message)
}
```

Now, we can finally run check to verify our QuickSort implementation. Lots of random arrays will be generated and passed to our test:

```
check("qsort should behave like sort") { (x: [Int]) in
    return qsort(x) == x.sort(<)
}
```

```
"qsort should behave like sort" passed 10 tests.
()
```

Using QuickCheck

Somewhat counterintuitively, there is strong evidence to suggest that testing technology influences the design of your code. People who rely on *test-driven design* use tests not only to verify that their code is correct. Instead, they also report that by writing your code in a test-driven fashion, the design of the code gets simpler. This makes sense — if it is easy to write a test for a class without having a complicated setup procedure, it means that the class is nicely decoupled.

For QuickCheck, the same rules apply. It will often not be easy to take existing code and add QuickCheck tests as an afterthought, particularly when you have an existing object-oriented architecture that relies heavily on other classes or makes use of mutable state. However, if you start by doing test-driven development using QuickCheck, you will see that it strongly influences the design of your code. QuickCheck forces you to think of the abstract properties that your functions must satisfy and allows you to give a high-level specification. A unit test can assert that 3 + 0 is equal to 0 + 3; a QuickCheck property states more generally that addition is a commutative operation. By thinking about a high-level QuickCheck specification first, your code is more likely to be biased toward modularity and *referential transparency* (which we will cover in the next chapter). QuickCheck does not work as well on stateful functions or APIs. As a result, writing your tests up front with QuickCheck will help keep your code clean.

Next Steps

This library is far from complete, but already quite useful. That said, there are a couple of obvious things that could be improved upon:

→ The shrinking is naive. For example, in the case of arrays, we currently remove the first element of the array. However, we might also choose to remove a different element, or make the elements of the array smaller (or do all of that). The current implementation returns an optional shrunken value, whereas we might want to generate a list of values. In a later chapter, we will see how to generate a lazy list of results, and we could use that same technique here.

→ The Arbitrary instances are quite simple. For different data types, we might want to have more complicated arbitrary instances. For example, when generating arbitrary enum values, we could generate certain cases with different frequencies. We could also generate constrained values, such as sorted or non-empty arrays. When writing multiple Arbitrary instances, it's possible to define some helper functions that aid us in writing these instances.

→ Classify the generated test data: if we generate a lot of arrays of length one, we could classify this as a 'trivial' test case. The Haskell library has support for classification, so these ideas could be ported directly.

→ We might want better control of the size of the random input that is generated. In the Haskell version of QuickCheck, the Arbitrary protocol takes an additional size argument, limiting the size of the random input generated; the check function than starts testing 'small' values, which

correspond to small and fast tests. As more and more tests pass, the
check function increases the size to try and find larger, more
complicated counterexamples.

→ We might also want to initialize the random generator with an explicit
seed, and make it possible to replay the generation of test cases. This
will make it easier to reproduce failing tests.

Obviously, that's not everything; there are many other small and large things
that could be improved upon to make this into a full library.

The Value of Immutability

Swift has several mechanisms for controlling how values may change. In this chapter, we will explain how these different mechanisms work, distinguish between value types and reference types, and argue why it is a good idea to limit the usage of mutable state.

Variables and References

In Swift, there are two ways to initialize a variable, using either **var** or **let**:

```
var x: Int = 1
let y: Int = 2
```

The crucial difference is that we can assign new values to variables declared using **var**, whereas variables created using **let** *cannot* change:

```
x = 3 // This is fine
y = 4 // This is rejected by the compiler
```

We will refer to variables declared using a **let** as *immutable* variables; variables declared using a **var**, on the other hand, are said to be *mutable*.

Why — you might wonder — would you ever declare an immutable variable? Doing so limits the variable's capabilities. A mutable variable is strictly more versatile. There is a clear case for preferring **var** over **let**. Yet in this section, we want to try and argue that the opposite is true.

Imagine having to read through a Swift class that someone else has written. There are a few methods that all refer to an instance variable with some meaningless name, say x. Given the choice, would you prefer x to be declared with a **var** or a **let**? Clearly declaring x to be immutable is preferable: you can read through the code without having to worry about what the *current* value of x is, you're free to substitute x for its definition, and you cannot invalidate x by assigning it some value that might break invariants on which the rest of the class relies.

Immutable variables may not be assigned a new value. As a result, it is *easier* to reason about immutable variables. In his famous paper, "Go To Statement Considered Harmful," Edsger Dijkstra writes:

> My... remark is that our intellectual powers are rather geared to master
> static relations and that our powers to visualize processes evolving in
> time are relatively poorly developed.

Dijkstra goes on to argue that the mental model a programmer needs to
develop when reading through structured code (using conditionals, loops, and
function calls, but not goto statements) is simpler than spaghetti code full of
gotos. We can take this discipline even further and eschew the use of mutable
variables: **var** considered harmful.

Value Types vs. Reference Types

The careful treatment of mutability is not present only in variable declarations.
Swift distinguishes between *value* types and *reference* types. The canonical
examples of value and reference types are structs and classes, respectively. To
illustrate the difference between value types and reference types, we will
define the following struct:

```
struct PointStruct {
    var x: Int
    var y: Int
}
```

Now consider the following code fragment:

```
var structPoint = PointStruct(x: 1, y: 2)
var sameStructPoint = structPoint
sameStructPoint.x = 3
```

After executing this code, sameStructPoint is clearly equal to (x: 3, y: 2).
However, structPoint still has its original value. This is the crucial distinction
between value types and reference types: when assigned to a new variable or
passed as an argument to a function, value types are copied. The assignment
to sameStructPoint.x does *not* update the original structPoint, because the
prior assignment, sameStructPoint = structPoint, has *copied* the value.

To further illustrate the difference, we could declare a class for points:

```
class PointClass {
    var x: Int
```

```
    var y: Int

    init (x: Int, y: Int) {
        self.x = x
        self.y = y
    }
}
```

Then we can adapt our code fragment from above to use this class instead:

```
var classPoint = PointClass(x: 1, y: 2)
var sameClassPoint = classPoint
sameClassPoint.x = 3
```

Now the assignment, sameClassPoint.x, modifies both classPoint and sameClassPoint, because classes are *reference* types. The distinction between value types and reference types is extremely important — you need to understand this distinction to predict how assignments modify data and which code may be affected by such changes.

The difference between value types and reference types is also apparent when calling functions. Consider the following (somewhat contrived) function that always returns the origin:

```
func setStructToOrigin(var point: PointStruct) -> PointStruct {
    point.x = 0
    point.y = 0
    return point
}
```

We use this function to compute a point:

```
var structOrigin: PointStruct = setStructToOrigin(structPoint)
```

All value types, such as structs, are copied when passed as function arguments. Therefore, in this example, the original structPoint is unmodified after the call to setStructToOrigin.

Now suppose we had written the following function, operating on classes rather than structs:

```
func setClassToOrigin(point: PointClass) -> PointClass {
    point.x = 0
    point.y = 0
```

```
    return point
}
```

Now the following function call *would* modify the classPoint:

```
var classOrigin = setClassToOrigin(classPoint)
```

When assigned to a new variable or passed to a function, value types are *always* copied, whereas reference types are *not*. Instead, a reference to the existing object or instance is used. Any changes to this reference will also mutate the original object or instance.

Andy Matuschak provides some very useful intuition for the difference between value types and reference types in his article for objc.io[1].

Structs are not the only value type in Swift. In fact, almost all the types in Swift are value types, including arrays, dictionaries, numbers, booleans, tuples, and enums (the latter will be covered in the coming chapter). Classes are the exception rather than the rule. This is one example of how Swift is moving away from object-oriented programming in favor of other programming paradigms.

We will discuss the relative merits of classes and structs later on in this section; before we do so, we want to briefly discuss the interaction between the different forms of mutability that we have seen thus far.

Structs and Classes: Mutable or Not?

In the examples above, we have declared all our points and their fields to be mutable, using **var** rather than **let**. The interaction between compound types, such as structs and classes, and the **var** and **let** declarations, requires some explanation.

Suppose we create the following immutable PointStruct:

```
let immutablePoint = PointStruct(x: 0, y: 0)
```

Of course, assigning a new value to this immutablePoint is not accepted:

1 https://objc.io/issues/16-swift/swift-classes-vs-structs/

```
immutablePoint = PointStruct(x: 1, y: 1) // Rejected
```

Similarly, trying to assign a new value to one of the point's properties is also rejected, although the properties in PointStruct have been defined as **var**, since immutablePoint is defined using **let**:

```
immutablePoint.x = 3 // Rejected
```

However, if we would have declared the point variable as mutable, we could change its components after initialization:

```
var mutablePoint = PointStruct(x: 1, y: 1)
mutablePoint.x = 3;
```

If we declare the x and y properties within the struct using the **let** keyword, then we can't ever change them after initialization, no matter whether the variable holding the point instance is mutable or immutable:

```
struct ImmutablePointStruct {
    let x: Int
    let y: Int
}
```

```
var immutablePoint2 = ImmutablePointStruct(x: 1, y: 1)
```

```
immutablePoint2.x = 3 // Rejected!
```

Of course, we can still assign a new value to immutablePoint2:

```
immutablePoint2 = ImmutablePointStruct(x: 2, y: 2)
```

Objective-C

The concept of mutability and immutability should already be familiar to many Objective-C programmers. Many of the data structures provided by Apple's Core Foundation and Foundation frameworks exist in immutable and mutable variants, such as NSArray and NSMutableArray, NSString and NSMutableString, and others. Using the immutable types is the default choice in most cases, just as Swift favors value types over reference types.

In contrast to Swift, however, there is no foolproof way to enforce immutability in Objective-C. We could declare the object's properties as read-only (or only expose an interface that avoids mutation), but this will not stop us from (unintentionally) mutating values internally after they have been initialized. When working with legacy code, for instance, it is all too easy to break assumptions about mutability that cannot be enforced by the compiler. Without checks by the compiler, it is very hard to enforce any kind of discipline in the use of mutable variables.

When dealing with framework code, we can often wrap existing mutable classes in a struct. However, we need to be careful here: if we store an object in a struct, the reference is immutable, but the object itself is not. Swift arrays work like this: they use a low-level mutable data structure, but provide an efficient and immutable interface. This is done using a technique called *copy-on-write*. You can read more about wrapping existing APIs in our book, Advanced Swift[2].

Discussion

In this chapter, we have seen how Swift distinguishes between mutable and immutable values, and between value types and reference types. In this final section, we want to explain *why* these are important distinctions.

When studying a piece of software, *coupling* measures the degree to which individual units of code depend on one another. Coupling is one of the single most important factors that determines how well software is structured. In the worst case, all classes and methods refer to one another, sharing numerous mutable variables, or even relying on exact implementation details. Such code can be very hard to maintain or update: instead of understanding or modifying a small code fragment in isolation, you constantly need to consider the system in its totality.

In Objective-C and many other object-oriented languages, it is common for methods to be coupled through shared instance variables. As a result, however, mutating the variable may change the behavior of the class's methods. Typically, this is a good thing — once you change the data stored in an object, all its methods may refer to its new value. At the same time, however, such shared instance variables introduce coupling between all the class's methods. If any of these methods or some external function invalidates the shared state, all the class's methods may exhibit buggy behavior. It is much harder to test any of these methods in isolation, as they are now coupled to one another.

2 https://objc.io/books/advanced-swift

Now compare this to the functions that we tested in the QuickCheck chapter. Each of these functions computed an output value that *only* depended on the input values. Such functions that compute the same output for equal inputs are sometimes called *referentially transparent*. By definition, referentially transparent methods are loosely coupled from their environments: there are no implicit dependencies on any state or variables, aside from the function's arguments. Consequently, referentially transparent functions are easier to test and understand in isolation. Furthermore, we can compose, call, and assemble functions that are referentially transparent without losing this property. Referential transparency is a guarantee of modularity and reusability.

Referential transparency increases modularity on all levels. Imagine reading through an API, trying to figure out how it works. The documentation may be sparse or out of date. But if you know the API is free of mutable state — all variables are declared using **let** rather than **var** — this is incredibly valuable information. You never need to worry about initializing objects or processing commands in exactly the right order. Instead, you can just look at types of the functions and constants that the API defines, and how these can be assembled to produce the desired value.

Swift's distinction between **var** and **let** enables programmers not only to distinguish between mutable and immutable data, but also to have the compiler enforce this distinction. Favoring **let** over **var** reduces the complexity of the program — you no longer have to worry about what the current value of mutable variables is, but can simply refer to their immutable definitions. Favoring immutability makes it easier to write referentially transparent functions, and ultimately, reduces coupling.

Similarly, Swift's distinction between value types and reference types encourages you to distinguish between mutable objects that may change and immutable data that your program manipulates. Functions are free to copy, change, or share values — any modifications will only ever affect their local copies. Once again, this helps write code that is more loosely coupled, as any dependencies resulting from shared state or objects can be eliminated.

Can we do without mutable variables entirely? Pure programming languages, such as Haskell, encourage programmers to avoid using mutable state altogether. There are certainly large Haskell programs that do not use any mutable state. In Swift, however, dogmatically avoiding **var** at all costs will not necessarily make your code better. There are plenty of situations where a function uses some mutable state internally. Consider the following example function that sums the elements of an array:

```
func sum(xs: [Int]) -> Int {
    var result = 0
    for x in xs {
        result += x
    }
    return result
}
```

The sum function uses a mutable variable, result, that is repeatedly updated. Yet the *interface* exposed to the user hides this fact. The sum function is still referentially transparent, and arguably easier to understand than a convoluted definition avoiding mutable variables at all costs. This example illustrates a *benign* usage of mutable state.

Such benign mutable variables have many applications. Consider the qsort method defined in the QuickCheck chapter:

```
func qsort(var array: [Int]) -> [Int] {
    if array.isEmpty { return [] }
    let pivot = array.removeAtIndex(0)
    let lesser = array. filter { $0 < pivot }
    let greater = array. filter { $0 >= pivot }
    return qsort(lesser) + [pivot] + qsort(greater)
}
```

Although this method mostly avoids using mutable references, it does not run in constant memory. It allocates new arrays, lesser and greater, which are combined to produce the final result. Of course, by using a mutable array, we can define a version of Quicksort that runs in constant memory and is still referentially transparent. Clever usage of mutable variables can sometimes improve performance or memory usage.

In summary, Swift offers several language features specifically designed to control the usage of mutable state in your program. It is almost impossible to avoid mutable state altogether, but mutation is used excessively and unnecessarily in many programs. Learning to avoid mutable state and objects whenever possible can help reduce coupling, thereby improving the structure of your code.

Enumerations

8

Throughout this book, we want to emphasize the important role *types* play in the design and implementation of Swift applications. In this chapter, we will describe Swift's *enumerations*, which enable you to craft precise types representing the data your application uses.

Introducing Enumerations

When creating a string, it is important to know its character encoding. In Objective-C, an NSString object can have several possible encodings:

```
enum NSStringEncoding {
    NSASCIIStringEncoding = 1,
    NSNEXTSTEPStringEncoding = 2,
    NSJapaneseEUCStringEncoding = 3,
    NSUTF8StringEncoding = 4,
    // ...
}
```

Each of these encodings is represented by a number; the **enum** allows programmers to assign meaningful names to the integer constants associated with particular character encoding.

There are some drawbacks to the enumeration declarations in Objective-C and other C dialects. Most notably, the type *NSStringEncoding* is not precise enough — there are integer values, such as 16, that do not correspond to a valid encoding. Furthermore, because all enumerated types are represented by integers, we can compute with them *as if they are numbers*, which is also a disadvantage:

```
NSAssert(NSASCIIStringEncoding + NSNEXTSTEPStringEncoding
        == NSJapaneseEUCStringEncoding, @"Adds up...");
```

Who would have thought that

```
NSASCIIStringEncoding + NSNEXTSTEPStringEncoding
```

is equal to NSJapaneseEUCStringEncoding? Such expressions are clearly nonsense, yet they are happily accepted by the Objective-C compiler.

Throughout the examples we have seen so far, we have used Swift's *type system* to catch such errors. Simply identifying enumerated types with integers is at odds with the one of core tenets of functional programming in Swift: using types effectively to rule out invalid programs.

Swift also has an **enum** construct, but it behaves very differently from the one you may be familiar with from Objective-C. We can declare our own enumerated type for string encodings as follows:

```
enum Encoding {
    case ASCII
    case NEXTSTEP
    case JapaneseEUC
    case UTF8
}
```

We have chosen to restrict ourselves to the first four possibilities defined in the NSStringEncoding enumeration listed above — there are many common encodings that we have not incorporated in this definition. This Swift enumeration declaration is for the purpose of illustration only. The Encoding type is inhabited by four possible values: ASCII, NEXTSTEP, JapaneseEUC, and UTF8. We will refer to the possible values of an enumeration as *member values*, or *members* for short. In a great deal of literature, such enumerations are sometimes called *sum types*. Throughout this book, however, we will use Apple's terminology.

In contrast to Objective-C, the following code is *not* accepted by the compiler:

```
let  myEncoding = Encoding.ASCII + Encoding.UTF8
```

Unlike Objective-C, enumerations in Swift create new types, distinct from integers or other existing types.

We can define functions that calculate with encodings using **switch** statements. For example, we may want to compute the NSStringEncoding corresponding to our encoding enumeration:

```
extension Encoding {
    var nsStringEncoding: NSStringEncoding {
        switch self {
            case .ASCII: return NSASCIIStringEncoding
            case .NEXTSTEP: return NSNEXTSTEPStringEncoding
            case .JapaneseEUC: return NSJapaneseEUCStringEncoding
            case .UTF8: return NSUTF8StringEncoding
        }
    }
```

```
}
```

This nsStringEncoding property maps each of the Encoding cases to the appropriate NSStringEncoding value. Note that we have one branch for each of our four different encoding schemes. If we leave any of these branches out, the Swift compiler warns us that the computed property's switch statement is not complete.

Of course, we can also define a function that works in the opposite direction, creating an Encoding from an NSStringEncoding. We'll implement this as an initializer on the Encoding enum:

```
extension `Encoding` {
    init ?(enc: NSStringEncoding) {
        switch enc {
            case NSASCIIStringEncoding: self = .ASCII
            case NSNEXTSTEPStringEncoding: self = .NEXTSTEP
            case NSJapaneseEUCStringEncoding: self = .JapaneseEUC
            case NSUTF8StringEncoding: self = .UTF8
            default: return nil
        }
    }
}
```

As we have not modeled all possible NSStringEncoding values in our little Encoding enumeration, the initializer is failable. If none of the first four cases succeed, the **default** branch is selected, which returns **nil**.

Of course, we do not need to use switch statements to work with our Encoding enumeration. For example, if we want the localized name of an encoding, we can compute it as follows:

```
func localizedEncodingName(encoding: Encoding) -> String {
    return .localizedNameOfStringEncoding(encoding.nsStringEncoding)
}
```

Associated Values

So far, we have seen how Swift's enumerations can be used to describe a choice between several different alternatives. The Encoding enumeration provided a safe, typed representation of different string encoding schemes. There are, however, many more applications of enumerations.

Recall the populationOfCapital function from Chapter 5. It looks up a country's capital, and if found, it returns the capital's population. The result type is an optional integer: if everything is found, the resulting population is returned. Otherwise, it is **nil**.

There is one drawback to using Swift's optional type: we do not return the error message when something goes wrong. This is rather unfortunate — if a call to populationOfCapital fails, there is no way to diagnose what went wrong. Does the country not exist in our dictionary? Is there no population defined for the capital?

Ideally, we would like our populationOfCapital function to return *either* an Int *or* an ErrorType. Using Swift's enumerations, we can do just that. Instead of returning an Int?, we will redefine our populationOfCapital function to return a member of the PopulationResult enumeration. We can define this enumeration as follows:

```
enum LookupError: ErrorType {
    case CapitalNotFound
    case PopulationNotFound
}

enum PopulationResult {
    case Success(Int)
    case Error(LookupError)
}
```

In contrast to the Encoding enumeration, the members of the PopulationResult have *associated values*. The PopulationResult has only two possible member values: Success and Error. In contrast to the Encoding enumeration, both of these member values carry additional information: the Success member has an integer associated with it, corresponding to the population of the country's capital; the Error member has an associated ErrorType. To illustrate this, we can declare an example Success member as follows:

```
let exampleSuccess: PopulationResult = .Success(1000)
```

Similarly, to create a PopulationResult result using the Error member, we would need to provide an associated LookupError value.

Now we can rewrite our populationOfCapital function to return a PopulationResult:

```
func populationOfCapital(country: String) -> PopulationResult {
    guard let capital = capitals[country] else {
        return .Error(.CapitalNotFound)
    }
    guard let population = cities[capital] else {
        return .Error(.PopulationNotFound)
    }
    return .Success(population)
}
```

Instead of returning an optional Int, we now return either the population or a LookupError. We first check if the capital is in the capitals dictionary; otherwise, we return a .CapitalNotFound error. Then we verify that there is a population in the cities. If not, we return a .PopulationNotFound error. Finally, if both the capital and population are found, we return a Success value.

Upon calling populationOfCapital, you can use a switch statement to determine whether or not the function succeeded:

```
switch populationOfCapital("France") {
  case let .Success(population):
      print("France's capital has \(population) thousand inhabitants")
  case let .Error(error):
      print("Error: \(error)")
}
```

Adding Generics

Let's say that we want to write a similar function to populationOfCapital, except instead of looking up the population, we want to look up the mayor of a country's capital:

```
let mayors = [
    "Paris": "Hidalgo",
    "Madrid": "Carmena",
    "Amsterdam": "van der Laan",
    "Berlin": "Müller"
]
```

By using optionals, we can simply look up the capital of the country and then flatMap over the result to find the mayor of that capital:

```
func mayorOfCapital(country: String) -> String? {
```

```
    return capitals[country].flatMap { mayors[$0] }
}
```

However, using an optional return type doesn't give us any information as to why the lookup failed.

But we now know how to solve this! Our first approach might be to reuse the PopulationResult enumeration to return the error. When mayorOfCapital succeeds, however, we do not have a string to associate with the Success member value. Instead, we have an integer. While we could convert the integer into a string, this indicates bad design: our types should be precise enough to prevent us from having to work with such conversions.

Alternatively, we can define a new enumeration, MayorResult, corresponding to the two possible cases:

```
enum MayorResult {
    case Success(Int)
    case Error(ErrorType)
}
```

We can certainly write a new version of the mayorOfCapital function using this enumeration — but introducing a new enumeration for each possible function seems tedious. Besides, the MayorResult and PopulationResult have an awful lot in common. The only difference between the two enumerations is the values associated with Success and Error. So we define a new enumeration that is *generic* in the result associated with Success and Failure:

```
enum Result<T> {
    case Success(T)
    case Error(ErrorType)
}
```

Now we can use the same result type for both populationOfCapital and mayorOfCapital. Their new type signatures become the following:

```
func populationOfCapital(country: String) -> Result<Int>
func mayorOfCapital(country: String) -> Result<String>
```

The populationOfCapital function returns either an Int or a LookupError; the mayorOfCapital function returns either a String or an ErrorType.

Swift Errors

Under the hood, Swift's built-in error handling works in a way very similar to the Result type we have defined above. They differ in two major ways: Swift forces you to annotate any code that might throw an error, and it forces you to use **try** (and variants) when calling code that might throw an error. With the Result type, we cannot statically guarantee this. A limitation of Swift's built-in mechanism is that it only works on the result type of a function: we cannot pass a possibly failed argument to a function (e.g. when providing a callback).

To rewrite our populationOfCapital function using Swift's errors, we simply add the **throws** keyword to the function's declaration. Instead of returning an .Error value, we now need to **throw** an error. Similarly, instead of returning a .Success value, we now just return the value directly:

```
func populationOfCapital1(country: String) throws -> Int {
    guard let capital = capitals[country] else {
        throw LookupError.CapitalNotFound
    }
    guard let population = cities[capital] else {
        throw LookupError.PopulationNotFound
    }
    return population
}
```

To call a function that is marked as **throws**, we can wrap the call in a **do**-block and add a **try** prefix. The advantage of this is that we can just write the regular flow within our **do**-block and handle all possible errors in the **catch**-block:

```
do {
    let population = try populationOfCapital1("France")
    print("France's population is \(population)")
} catch {
    print("Lookup error: \(error)")
}
```

Optionals Revisited

Under the hood, Swift's built-in optional type is very similar to the Result type that we've defined here. The following snippet is taken almost directly from the Swift standard library:

```
enum Optional<T> {
    case None
    case Some(T)
    // ...
}
```

The optional type just provides some syntactic sugar, such as the postfix ? notation and optional unwrapping mechanism, to make it easier to use. There is, however, no reason that you couldn't define it yourself.

In fact, we can even define some of the library functions for manipulating optionals on our own Result type. For example, we can redefine the ?? operator to work on our Result type:

```
func ??<T>(result: Result<T>, handleError: ErrorType -> T) -> T {
    switch result {
        case let .Success(value):
            return value
        case let .Error(error):
            return handleError(error)
    }
}
```

The Algebra of Data Types

As we mentioned previously, enumerations are often referred to as sum types. This may be a confusing name, as enumerations seem to have no relation to numbers. Yet if you dig a little deeper, you may find that enumerations and tuples have mathematical structure, very similar to arithmetic.

Before we explore this structure, we need to consider the question of when two types are the same. This may seem like a very strange question to ask — isn't it obvious that String and String are equal, but String and Int are not? However, as soon as you add generics, enumerations, structs, and functions to the mix, the answer is not so obvious. Such a simple question is still the subject of active research exploring the very foundations of mathematics[1]. For the purpose of this subsection, we will study when two types are *isomorphic*.

---

[1] http://homotopytypetheory.org

Intuitively, the two types A and B are isomorphic if we can convert between them without losing any information. We need to have two functions, f: A -> B and g: B -> A, which are the inverse of one another. More specifically, for x: A, the result of calling g(f(x)) must be equal to x; similarly, for all y: B, the result of f(g(y)) must be equal to y. This definition crystallizes the intuition we stated above: we can convert freely between the types A and B using f and g, without ever losing information (as we can always undo f using g, and vice versa). This definition is not precise enough for most programming purposes — 64 bits can be used to represent Integers or memory addresses, even if these are two very different concepts. They will be useful, however, as we study the algebraic structure of types.

To begin with, consider the following enumeration:

```
enum Add<T, U> {
    case InLeft(T)
    case InRight(U)
}
```

Given two types, T and U, the enumeration Add<T, U> consists of either a value of type T, or a value of type U. As its name suggests, the Add enumeration adds together the members from the types T and U: if T has three members and U has seven, Add<T, U> will have ten possible members. This observation provides some further insight into why enumerations are called sum types.

In arithmetic, zero is the unit of addition, i.e., x + 0 is the same as using just x for any number x. Can we find an enumeration that behaves like zero? Interestingly, Swift allows us to define the following enumeration:

```
enum Zero { }
```

This enumeration is empty — it doesn't have any members. As we hoped, this enumeration behaves exactly like the zero of arithmetic: for any type T, the types Add<T, Zero> and T are isomorphic. It is fairly easy to prove this. We can use InLeft to define a function converting T to Add<T,Zero>, and the conversion in the other direction can be done by pattern matching.

So much for addition — let us now consider multiplication. If we have an enumeration, T, with three members, and another enumeration, U, with two members, how can we define a compound type, Times<T, U>, with six members? To do this, the Times<T, U> type should allow you to choose *both* a member of T and a member of U. In other words, it should correspond to a pair of two values of type T and U respectively:

```
struct Times<T, U> {
    let fst: T
    let snd: U
}
```

Just as Zero was the unit of addition, the void type, $()$, is the unit of Times:

```
typealias One = ()
```

It is easy to check that many familiar laws from arithmetic are still valid when read as isomorphisms between types:

→ Times<One, T> is isomorphic to T

→ Times<Zero, T> is isomorphic to Zero

→ Times<T, U> is isomorphic to Times<U, T>

Types defined using enumerations and tuples are sometimes referred to as *algebraic data types*, because they have this algebraic structure, similar to natural numbers.

This correspondence between numbers and types runs much deeper than we have sketched here. Functions can be shown to correspond to exponentiation. There is even a notion of differentiation[2] that can be defined on types!

This observation may not be of much practical value. Rather it shows how enumerations, like many of Swift's features, are not new, but instead draw on years of research in mathematics and program language design.

Why Use Enumerations?

Working with optionals may still be preferable over the Result type that we have defined here, for a variety of reasons: the built-in syntactic sugar can be convenient; the interface you define will be more familiar to Swift developers, as you only rely on existing types instead of defining your own enumeration; and sometimes the ErrorType is not worth the additional hassle of defining an enumeration.

---

2 http://strictlypositive.org/calculus

The point we want to make, however, is not that the Result type is the best way to handle all errors in Swift. Instead, we hope to illustrate how you can use enumerations to define your own types, tailored to your specific needs. By making these types precise, you can use Swift's type checking to your advantage and prevent many bugs, before your program has been tested or run.

Purely
Functional Data
Structures

In the previous chapter, we saw how to use enumerations to define specific types tailored to the application you are developing. In this chapter, we will define *recursive* enumerations and show how these can be used to define data structures that are both efficient and persistent.

Binary Search Trees

When Swift was released, it did not have a library for manipulating sets, like Objective-C's NSSet library. While we could have written a Swift wrapper around NSSet — like we did for Core Image and the String initializer — we will instead explore a slightly different approach. Our aim is, once again, not to define a complete library for manipulating sets in Swift, but rather to demonstrate how recursive enumerations can be used to define efficient data structures.

In our little library, we will implement the following four operations:

- → empty — returns an empty set
- → isEmpty — checks whether or not a set is empty
- → contains — checks whether or not an element is in a set
- → insert — adds an element to an existing set

As a first attempt, we may use arrays to represent sets. These four operations are almost trivial to implement:

```
func empty<Element>() -> [Element] {
    return []
}

func isEmpty<Element>(set: [Element]) -> Bool {
    return set.isEmpty
}

func contains<Element: Equatable>(x: Element, _ set: [Element]) -> Bool {
    return set.contains(x)
}

func insert<Element: Equatable>(x: Element, _ set:[Element]) -> [Element] {
    return contains(x, set) ? set : [x] + set
}
```

While simple, the drawback of this implementation is that many of the operations perform linearly in the size of the set. For large sets, this may cause performance problems.

There are several possible ways to improve performance. For example, we could ensure the array is sorted and use binary search to locate specific elements. Instead, we will define a *binary search tree* to represent our sets. We can build a tree structure in the traditional C style, maintaining pointers to subtrees at every node. However, we can also define such trees directly as an enumeration in Swift using the **indirect** keyword:

```
indirect enum BinarySearchTree<Element: Comparable> {
    case Leaf
    case Node(BinarySearchTree<Element>, Element, BinarySearchTree<Element>)
}
```

This definition states that every tree is either:

→ a Leaf without associated values, or

→ a Node with three associated values, which are the left subtree, a value stored at the node, and the right subtree.

Before defining functions on trees, we can write a few example trees by hand:

```
let leaf: BinarySearchTree<Int> = .Leaf
```

```
let five: BinarySearchTree<Int> = .Node(leaf, 5, leaf)
```

The leaf tree is empty; the five tree stores the value 5 at a node, but both subtrees are empty. We can generalize these constructions with two initializers: one that builds an empty tree, and one that builds a tree with a single value:

```
extension BinarySearchTree {
    init () {
        self = .Leaf
    }

    init (_ value: Element) {
        self = .Node(.Leaf, value, .Leaf)
    }
}
```

Just as we saw in the previous chapter, we can write functions that manipulate trees using switch statements. As the BinarySearchTree enumeration itself is recursive, it should come as no surprise that many functions we write over trees will also be recursive. For example, the following function counts the number of elements stored in a tree:

```
extension BinarySearchTree {
    var count: Int {
        switch self {
        case .Leaf:
            return 0
        case let .Node(left, _, right):
            return 1 + left.count + right.count
        }
    }
}
```

In the base case for leaves, we can return 0 immediately. The case for nodes is more interesting: we compute the number of elements stored in both subtrees *recursively*. We then return their sum and add 1 to account for the value stored at this node.

Similarly, we can write an elements property that computes the array of elements stored in a tree:

```
extension BinarySearchTree {
    var elements: [Element] {
        switch self {
        case .Leaf:
            return []
        case let .Node(left, x, right):
            return left.elements + [x] + right.elements
        }
    }
}
```

Now let's return to our original goal, which is writing an efficient set library using trees. We have an obvious choice for checking whether or not a tree is empty:

```
extension BinarySearchTree {
    var isEmpty: Bool {
        if case .Leaf = self {
            return true
```

```
        }
        return false
    }
}
```

If we try to write naive versions of insert and contains, however, it seems that we have not gained much. But if we restrict ourselves to *binary search trees*, we can perform much better. A (non-empty) tree is said to be a binary search tree if all of the following conditions are met:

→ all the values stored in the left subtree are *less* than the value stored at the root

→ all the values stored in the right subtree are *greater* than the value stored at the root

→ both the left and right subtrees are binary search trees

The way we implement the BinarySearchTree in this chapter comes with a disadvantage: we cannot strictly enforce the tree to be a binary search tree, because you can just construct any tree "by hand." In the real world, we should encapsulate the enum as a private implementation detail so that we can guarantee the tree to be a binary search tree. We omit this here for the sake of simplicity.

We can write an (inefficient) check to ascertain if a BinarySearchTree is in fact a binary search tree:

```
extension BinarySearchTree where Element: Comparable {
    var isBST: Bool {
        switch self {
        case .Leaf:
            return true
        case let .Node(left, x, right):
            return left.elements.all { y in y < x }
                && right.elements.all { y in y > x }
                && left.isBST
                && right.isBST
        }
    }
}
```

The all function checks if a property holds for all elements in an array. It is defined as an extension on SequenceType:

```
extension SequenceType {
    func all (predicate: Generator.Element -> Bool) -> Bool {
        for x in self where !predicate(x) {
            return false
        }
        return true
    }
}
```

The crucial property of binary search trees is that they admit an efficient lookup operation, akin to binary search in an array. As we traverse the tree to determine whether or not an element is in the tree, we can rule out (up to) half of the remaining elements in every step. For example, here is one possible definition of the contains function that determines whether or not an element occurs in the tree:

```
extension BinarySearchTree {
    func contains(x: Element) -> Bool {
        switch self {
        case .Leaf:
            return false
        case let .Node(_, y, _) where x == y:
            return true
        case let .Node(left, y, _) where x < y:
            return left.contains(x)
        case let .Node(_, y, right) where x > y:
            return right.contains(x)
        default:
            fatalError("The impossible occurred")
        }
    }
}
```

The contains function now distinguishes four possible cases:

→ If the tree is empty, the x is not in the tree and we return false.

→ If the tree is non-empty and the value stored at its root is equal to x, we return true.

→ If the tree is non-empty and the value stored at its root is greater than x, we know that if x is in the tree, it must be in the left subtree. Hence, we recursively search for x in the left subtree.

→ Similarly, if x is greater than the value stored at the root, we proceed by searching the right subtree.

Unfortunately, the Swift compiler is not yet clever enough to see that these four cases cover all the possibilities, so we need to insert a dummy default case.

Insertion searches through the binary search tree in exactly the same fashion:

```
extension BinarySearchTree {
    mutating func insert(x: Element) {
        switch self {
        case .Leaf:
            self = BinarySearchTree(x)
        case .Node(var left, let y, var right):
            if x < y { left.insert(x) }
            if x > y { right.insert(x) }
            self = .Node(left, y, right)
        }
    }
}
```

Instead of checking first whether or not the element is already contained in the binary search tree, insert finds a suitable location to add the new element. If the tree is empty, it builds a tree with a single element. If the element is already present, it returns the original tree. Otherwise, the insert function continues recursively, navigating to a suitable location to insert the new element.

The insert function is written as a **mutating** function. However, this is very different from mutation — for example, in a class-based data structure. The actual *values* are not mutated, just the variables. For example, in the case of insertion, the new tree is constructed out of the branches of the old tree. These branches never get mutated. We can verify this behavior by looking at a usage example:

```
let myTree: BinarySearchTree<Int> = BinarySearchTree()
var copied = myTree
copied.insert(5)
(myTree.elements, copied.elements)
```

```
([], [5])
```

The worst-case performance of insert and contains on binary search trees is still linear — after all, we could have a very unbalanced tree, where every left subtree is empty. More clever implementations, such as 2-3 trees, AVL trees, or red-black trees, avoid this by maintaining the invariant that each tree is suitably balanced. Furthermore, we haven't written a delete operation, which would also require rebalancing. These are tricky operations for which there are plenty of well-documented implementations in the literature — once again, this example serves as an illustration of working with recursive enumerations and does not pretend to be a complete library.

Autocompletion Using Tries

Now that we've seen binary trees, this last section will cover a more advanced and purely functional data structure. Suppose that we want to write our own autocompletion algorithm — given a history of searches and the prefix of the current search, we should compute an array of possible completions.

Using arrays, the solution is entirely straightforward:

```
func autocomplete(history: [String], textEntered: String) -> [String] {
    return history. filter  { $0.hasPrefix(textEntered) }
}
```

Unfortunately, this function is not very efficient. For large histories and long prefixes, it may be too slow. Once again, we could improve performance by keeping the history sorted and using some kind of binary search on the history array. Instead, we will explore a different solution, using a custom data structure tailored for this kind of query.

Tries, also known as digital search trees, are a particular kind of ordered tree. Typically, tries are used to look up a string, which consists of a list of characters. Instead of storing strings in a binary search tree, it can be more efficient to store them in a structure that repeatedly branches over the strings' constituent characters.

Previously, the BinarySearchTree type had two subtrees at every node. Tries, on the other hand, do not have a fixed number of subtrees at every node, but instead (potentially) have subtrees for every character. For example, we could visualize a trie storing the string "cat," "car," "cart," and "dog" as follows:

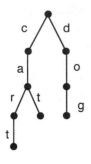

Figure 9.1: Trie

To determine if the string "care" is in the trie, we follow the path from the root, along the edges labeled 'c,' 'a,' and 'r.' As the node labeled 'r' does not have a child labeled with 'e,' the string "care" is not in this trie. The string "cat" is in the trie, as we can follow a path from the root along edges labeled 'c,' 'a,' and 't.'

How can we represent such tries in Swift? As a first attempt, we write a struct storing a dictionary, mapping characters to subtries at every node:

```
struct Trie {
    let children: [Character: Trie]
}
```

There are two improvements we would like to make to this definition. First of all, we need to add some additional information to the node. From the example trie above, you can see that by adding "cart" to the trie, all the prefixes of "cart" — namely "c," "ca," and "car" — also appear in the trie. As we may want to distinguish between prefixes that are or are not in the trie, we will add an additional boolean, isElement, to every node. This boolean indicates whether or not the current string is in the trie. Finally, we can define a generic trie that is no longer restricted to only storing characters. Doing so yields the following definition of tries:

```
struct Trie<Element: Hashable> {
    let isElement: Bool
    let children: [Element: Trie<Element>]
}
```

In the text that follows, we will sometimes refer to the keys of type [Element] as strings, and values of type Element as characters. This is not very precise — as Element can be instantiated with a type different than characters, and a string is not the same as [Character] — but we hope it does appeal to the intuition of tries storing a collection of strings.

Before defining our autocomplete function on tries, we will write a few simple definitions to warm up. For example, the empty trie consists of a node with an empty dictionary:

```
extension Trie {
    init () {
        isElement = false
        children = [:]
    }
}
```

If we had chosen to set the isElement boolean stored in the empty trie to **true** rather than **false**, the empty string would be a member of the empty trie — which is probably not the behavior that we want.

Next, we define a property to flatten a trie into an array containing all its elements:

```
extension Trie {
    var elements: [[Element]] {
        var result: [[Element]] = isElement ? [[]]  :  []
        for (key, value) in children {
            result += value.elements.map { [key] + $0 }
        }
        return result
    }
}
```

This function is a bit tricky. It starts by checking whether or not the current root is marked as a member of the trie. If it is, the trie contains the empty key; if it is not, the result variable is initialized to the empty array. Next, it traverses the dictionary, computing the elements of the subtries — this is done by the call to value.elements. Finally, the 'character' associated with every subtrie is added to the front of the elements of that subtrie — this is taken care of by the map function. We could have written this with a flatMap instead of a **for** loop, but we believe the code is a bit clearer like this.

Next, we would like to define lookup and insertion functions. Before we do so, however, we will need a few auxiliary functions. We have represented keys as an array. While our tries are defined as (recursive) structs, arrays are not. Yet it can still be useful to traverse an array recursively. To make this a bit easier, we define the following extension on arrays:

```
extension Array {
    var decompose: (Element, [Element])? {
        return isEmpty ? nil : (self[startIndex], Array(self.dropFirst()))
    }
}
```

The decompose function checks whether or not an array is empty. If it is empty, it returns **nil**; if the array is not empty, it returns a tuple containing both the first element of the array and the tail or remainder of the array, with the first element removed. We can recursively traverse an array by repeatedly calling decompose until it returns **nil** and the array is empty.

For example, we can use the decompose function to sum the elements of an array recursively, without using a **for** loop or reduce:

```
func sum(xs: [Int]) -> Int {
    guard let (head, tail) = xs.decompose else { return 0 }
    return head + sum(tail)
}
```

Another less obvious example for a recursive implementation using decompose is to rewrite our qsort function from Chapter 6:

```
func qsort(input: [Int]) -> [Int] {
    guard let (pivot, rest) = input.decompose else { return [] }
    let lesser = rest.filter { $0 < pivot }
    let greater = rest.filter { $0 >= pivot }
    return qsort(lesser) + [pivot] + qsort(greater)
}
```

Back to our original problem — we can now use the decompose helper on arrays to write a lookup function that, given an array of Elements, traverses a trie to determine whether or not the corresponding key is stored:

```
extension Trie {
    func lookup(key: [Element]) -> Bool {
        guard let (head, tail) = key.decompose else { return isElement }
        guard let subtrie = children[head] else { return false }
        return subtrie.lookup(tail)
    }
}
```

Here we can distinguish three cases:

→ The key is empty — in this case, we return isElement, the boolean indicating whether or not the string described by the current node is in the trie.

→ The key is non-empty, but the corresponding subtrie does not exist — in this case, we simply return **false**, as the key is not included in the trie.

→ The key is non-empty — in this case, we look up the subtrie corresponding to the first element of the key. If this also exists, we make a recursive call, looking up the tail of the key in this subtrie.

We can adapt lookup to return the subtrie, containing all the elements that have some prefix:

```
extension Trie {
    func withPrefix(prefix: [Element]) -> Trie<Element>? {
        guard let (head, tail) = prefix.decompose else { return self }
        guard let remainder = children[head] else { return nil }
        return remainder.withPrefix(tail)
    }
}
```

The only difference with the lookup function is that we no longer return the isElement boolean, but instead return the whole subtrie, containing all the elements with the argument prefix.

Finally, we can redefine our autocomplete function to use the more efficient tries data structure:

```
extension Trie {
    func autocomplete(key: [Element]) -> [[Element]] {
        return withPrefix(key)?.elements ?? []
    }
}
```

To compute all the strings in a trie with a given prefix, we simply call the withPrefix function and extract the elements from the resulting trie, if it exists. If there is no subtrie with the given prefix, we simply return an empty array.

We can use the same pattern of decomposing the key to create tries. For example, we can create a new trie storing only a single element, as follows:

```
extension Trie {
```

```
init (_ key: [Element]) {
    if let (head, tail) = key.decompose {
        let children = [head: Trie(tail)]
        self = Trie(isElement: false, children: children)
    } else {
        self = Trie(isElement: true, children: [:])
    }
}
}
```

Once again, we distinguish two cases:

→ If the input key is non-empty and can be decomposed in a head and tail, we recursively create a trie from the tail. We then create a new dictionary of children, storing this trie at the head entry. Finally, we create the trie from the dictionary, and as the input key is non-empty, we set isElement to **false**.

→ If the input key is empty, we create a new empty trie, storing the empty string (isElement: **true**) with no children.

To populate a trie, we define the following insertion function:

```
extension Trie {
    func insert(key: [Element]) -> Trie<Element> {
        guard let (head, tail) = key.decompose else {
            return Trie(isElement: true, children: children)
        }
        var newChildren = children
        if let nextTrie = children[head] {
            newChildren[head] = nextTrie.insert(tail)
        } else {
            newChildren[head] = Trie(tail)
        }
        return Trie(isElement: isElement, children: newChildren)
    }
}
```

The insertion function distinguishes three cases:

→ If the key is empty, we set isElement to **true** and leave the remainder of trie unmodified.

→ If the key is non-empty and the head of the key already occurs in the children dictionary at the current node, we simply make a recursive call, inserting the tail of the key in the next trie.

→ If the key is non-empty and its first element, head, does not yet have an entry in the trie's children dictionary, we create a new trie storing the remainder of the key. To complete the insertion, we associate this trie with the head key at the current node.

As an exercise, you can rewrite the insert as a **mutating** function.

String Tries

In order to use our autocompletion algorithm, we can now write a few wrappers that make working with string tries a bit easier. First, we can write a simple wrapper to build a trie from a list of words. It starts with the empty trie and then inserts each word, yielding a trie with all the words combined. Because our tries work on arrays, we need to convert every string into an array of characters. Alternatively, we could write a variant of insert that works on any SequenceType:

```
func buildStringTrie(words: [String]) -> Trie<Character> {
    let emptyTrie = Trie<Character>()
    return words.reduce(emptyTrie) { trie, word in
        trie.insert(Array(word.characters))
    }
}
```

Finally, to get a list of all our autocompleted words, we can call our previously defined autocomplete function, turning the result back into strings. Note how we prepend the input string to each result. This is because the autocomplete function only returns the rest of the word, excluding the common prefix:

```
func autocompleteString(knownWords: Trie<Character>, word: String) -> [String] {
    let chars = Array(word.characters)
    let completed = knownWords.autocomplete(chars)
    return completed.map { chars in
        word + String(chars)
    }
}
```

To test our functions, we can use a simple list of words, build a trie, and list the autocompletions:

```
let contents = ["cat", "car", "cart", "dog"]
let trieOfWords = buildStringTrie(contents)
autocompleteString(trieOfWords, word: "car")
```

```
["car", "cart"]
```

Currently, our interface only allows us to insert arrays. It is easy to create an alternative insert function that allows us to insert any kind of collection. The type signature would be more complicated, but the body of the function would stay the same.

```
func insert<Seq: CollectionType where Seq.Generator.Element == Element>
    (key: Seq) -> Trie<Element>
```

This chapter comes with a sample project (available on GitHub[1]) that loads all the words from /usr/share/dict/words and builds a trie of them using the buildStringTrie function above. Building up a trie of almost 250,000 words takes up quite a bit of time. However, we could optimize this by writing an alternative function to build a trie from an already sorted list of words. This is also highly parallelizable; it would be possible to build the trie for all words, starting with letters from 'a' to 'm,' and the letters from 'n' to 'z' in parallel, and combining the results.

It is very easy to make the Trie data type conform to SequenceType, which will add a lot of functionality: it automatically provides functions like contains, filter , map, and reduce on the elements. We will look in more detail at SequenceType in the chapter on generators and sequences.

Discussion

These are but two examples of writing efficient, immutable data structures using enumerations and structs. There are many others in Chris Okasaki's *Purely Functional Data Structures* (1999), which is a standard reference on the subject. Interested readers may also want to read Ralf Hinze and Ross Paterson's work on finger trees (2006), which are general-purpose purely functional data structures with numerous applications. Finally, StackOverflow[2] has a fantastic list of more recent research in this area.

---

1 https://github.com/objcio/functional-swift
2 http:
    //cstheory.stackexchange.com/questions/1539/whats-new-in-purely-functional-data-structures-since-okasaki

Case Study:
Diagrams

10

In this chapter, we'll look at a functional way to describe diagrams and discuss how to draw them with Core Graphics. By wrapping Core Graphics with a functional layer, we get an API that's simpler and more composable.

Drawing Squares and Circles

Imagine drawing the diagram in Figure 10.1. In Core Graphics, we could achieve this drawing with the following commands:

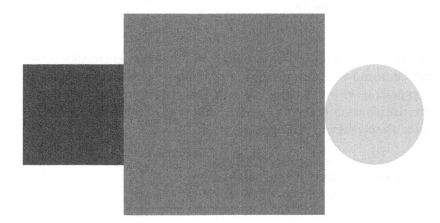

Figure 10.1: A simple diagram

```
NSColor.blueColor().setFill()
CGContextFillRect(context, CGRectMake(0.0, 37.5, 75.0, 75.0))
NSColor.redColor().setFill()
CGContextFillRect(context, CGRectMake(75.0, 0.0, 150.0, 150.0))
NSColor.greenColor().setFill()
CGContextFillEllipseInRect(context, CGRectMake(225.0, 37.5, 75.0, 75.0))
```

This is nice and short, but it is a bit difficult to maintain. For example, what if we wanted to add an extra circle like in Figure 10.2?

Figure 10.2: Adding an extra circle

We would need to add the code for drawing a circle and also update the drawing code to move some of the other objects to the right. In Core Graphics, we always describe *how* to draw things. In this chapter, we'll build a library for diagrams that allows us to express *what* we want to draw. For example, the first diagram can be expressed like this:

```
let blueSquare = square(side: 1).fill(. blueColor())
let redSquare = square(side: 2).fill(. redColor())
let greenCircle = circle(diameter: 1). fill (. greenColor())
let example1 = blueSquare ||| redSquare ||| greenCircle
```

Adding the second circle is as simple as changing the last line of code:

```
let cyanCircle = circle(diameter: 1). fill (. cyanColor())
let example2 = blueSquare ||| cyanCircle ||| redSquare ||| greenCircle
```

The code above first describes a blue square with a relative size of 1. The red square is twice as big (it has a relative size of 2). We compose the diagram by putting the squares and the circle next to each other with the ||| operator. Changing this diagram is very simple, and there's no need to worry about calculating frames or moving things around. The examples describe *what* should be drawn, not *how* it should be drawn.

In the chapter about thinking functionally, we've constructed regions by composing simple functions. While it served us well to illustrate functional programming concepts, this approach has one decisive drawback: we can't inspect *how* a region has been constructed — we can only check whether or not a point is included.

In this chapter we'll go one step further: instead of immediately executing the drawing commands, we build an intermediate data structure that describes the diagram. This is a very powerful technique; contrary to the regions example, it allows us to inspect the data structure, modify it, and convert it into different formats.

As a more complex example of a diagram generated by the same library, Figure 10.3 shows a bar graph:

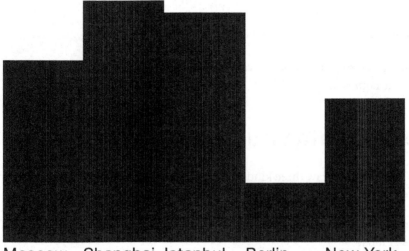

Figure 10.3: A bar graph

We can write a barGraph function that takes a list of names (the keys) and values (the relative heights of the bars). For each value in the dictionary, we draw a suitably sized rectangle. We then horizontally concatenate these rectangles with the hcat function. Finally, we put the bars and the text below each other using the --- operator:

```
func barGraph(input: [(String, Double)]) -> Diagram {
    let values: [CGFloat] = input.map { CGFloat($0.1) }
    let nValues = values.normalize()
    let bars = hcat(nValues.map { (x: CGFloat) -> Diagram in
        return rect(width: 1, height: 3 * x) . fill (. blackColor()).alignBottom()
        })
    let labels = hcat(input.map { x in
        return text(x.0, width: 1, height: 0.3).alignTop()
```

```
        })
    return bars --- labels
}

let cities = [
    "Shanghai": 14.01,
    "Istanbul": 13.3,
    "Moscow": 10.56,
    "New York": 8.33,
    "Berlin": 3.43
]

let example3 = barGraph(Array(cities))
```

The normalized function used above simply normalizes all values so that the largest one equals one.

The Core Data Structures

In our library, we'll draw three kinds of things: ellipses, rectangles, and text. Using enums, we can define a data type for these three possibilities:

```
enum Primitive {
    case Ellipse
    case Rectangle
    case Text(String)
}
```

Diagrams are defined using an enum as well. First, a diagram could be a primitive, which has a size and is either an ellipse, a rectangle, or text. Note that we call it Prim because, at the time of writing, the compiler gets confused by a case that has the same name as another enum:

```
case Prim(CGSize, Primitive)
```

Then, we have cases for diagrams that are beside each other (horizontally) or below each other (vertically). Note how a Beside diagram is defined recursively — it consists of two diagrams next to each other:

```
case Beside(Diagram, Diagram)
case Below(Diagram, Diagram)
```

To style diagrams, we'll add a case for attributed diagrams. This allows us to set the fill color (for example, for ellipses and rectangles). We'll define the Attribute type later:

case Attributed(Attribute, Diagram)

The last case is for alignment. Suppose we have a small rectangle and a large rectangle that are next to each other. By default, the small rectangle gets centered vertically, as seen in Figure 10.4:

Figure 10.4: Vertical centering

But by adding a case for alignment, we can control the alignment of smaller parts of the diagram:

case Align(CGVector, Diagram)

For example, Figure 10.5 shows a diagram that's top aligned. It is drawn using the following code:

Figure 10.5: Vertical alignment

Diagram.Align(CGVector(dx: 0.5, dy: 1), blueSquare) ||| redSquare

We can define Diagram as a recursive enum. Just like with the Tree enum, we need to mark it as **indirect**:

```
indirect enum Diagram {
    case Prim(CGSize, Primitive)
    case Beside(Diagram, Diagram)
    case Below(Diagram, Diagram)
    case Attributed(Attribute, Diagram)
    case Align(CGVector, Diagram)
}
```

The Attribute enum is a data type for describing different attributes of diagrams. Currently, it only supports FillColor, but it could easily be extended to support attributes for stroking, gradients, text attributes, etc.:

```
enum Attribute {
    case FillColor(NSColor)
}
```

Calculating and Drawing

Calculating the size for the Diagram data type is easy. The only cases that aren't straightforward are for Beside and Below. In case of Beside, the width is equal to the sum of the widths, and the height is equal to the maximum height of the left and right diagram. For Below, it's a similar pattern. For all the other cases, we just call size recursively:

```
extension Diagram {
    var size: CGSize {
        switch self {
        case .Prim(let size, _):
            return size
        case .Attributed(_, let x):
            return x.size
        case .Beside(let l, let r):
            let sizeL = l.size
            let sizeR = r.size
            return CGSizeMake(sizeL.width + sizeR.width,
                max(sizeL.height, sizeR.height))
        case .Below(let l, let r):
            return CGSizeMake(max(l.size.width, r.size.width),
                l.size.height + r.size.height)
        case .Align(_, let r):
            return r.size
        }
    }
}
```

Before we start drawing, we will first define one more function. The fit function works on an input size (i.e. the size of a diagram), and it takes an alignment vector (which we used in the Align case of a diagram) and a rectangle that we want to fit the input size into. The input size is defined relatively to the other elements in our diagram. We scale the input size up and maintain its aspect ratio:

```
extension CGSize {
    func fit (vector: CGVector, _ rect: CGRect) -> CGRect {
        let scaleSize = rect.size / self
        let scale = min(scaleSize.width, scaleSize.height)
        let size = scale * self
        let space = vector.size * (size - rect.size)
        return CGRect(origin: rect.origin - space.point, size: size)
    }
```

```
}
```

In order to be able to write the calculations in the fit function in an expressive way, we've defined the following operators and helper functions on CGSize, CGPoint, and CGVector:

```
func *(l: CGFloat, r: CGSize) -> CGSize {
    return CGSize(width: l * r.width, height: l * r.height)
}
func /(l: CGSize, r: CGSize) -> CGSize {
    return CGSize(width: l.width / r.width, height: l.height / r.height)
}
func *(l: CGSize, r: CGSize) -> CGSize {
    return CGSize(width: l.width * r.width, height: l.height * r.height)
}
func -(l: CGSize, r: CGSize) -> CGSize {
    return CGSize(width: l.width - r.width, height: l.height - r.height)
}
func -(l: CGPoint, r: CGPoint) -> CGPoint {
    return CGPoint(x: l.x - r.x, y: l.y - r.y)
}

extension CGSize {
    var point: CGPoint {
        return CGPoint(x: self.width, y: self.height)
    }
}

extension CGVector {
    var point: CGPoint { return CGPoint(x: dx, y: dy) }
    var size: CGSize { return CGSize(width: dx, height: dy) }
}
```

Let's try out the fit function. For example, if we fit and center a square of 1x1 into a rectangle of 200x100, we get the following result:

```
CGSize(width: 1, height: 1). fit (
    CGVector(dx: 0.5, dy: 0.5), CGRect(x: 0, y: 0, width: 200, height: 100))

// (50.0, 0.0, 100.0, 100.0)
```

To align the rectangle to the left, we would do the following:

```
CGSize(width: 1, height: 1). fit (
```

```
CGVector(dx: 0, dy: 0.5), CGRect(x: 0, y: 0, width: 200, height: 100))
```

```
// (0.0, 0.0, 100.0, 100.0)
```

Now that we can represent diagrams and calculate their sizes, we're ready to draw them. We use pattern matching to make it easy to know what to draw. Because we will always draw in the same context, we define it as an extension of CGContextRef. The draw method takes two parameters: the bounds to draw in, and the actual diagram. Given the bounds, the diagram will try to fit itself into the bounds using the fit function defined before. For example, when we draw an ellipse, we center it and make it fill the available bounds:

For rectangles, this is almost the same, except that we call a different Core Graphics function. You might note that the frame calculation is the same as for ellipses. It would be possible to pull this out and have a nested switch statement, but we think the following is more readable when presenting in book form:

```
case .Prim(let size, .Rectangle):
    let frame = size.fit(CGVector(dx: 0.5, dy: 0.5), bounds)
    CGContextFillRect(self, frame)
```

In the current version of our library, all text is set in the system font with a fixed size. It's very possible to make this an attribute or change the Text primitive to make this configurable. In its current form though, drawing text works like this:

```
case .Prim(let size, .Text(let text)):
    let frame = size.fit(CGVector(dx: 0.5, dy: 0.5), bounds)
    let font = NSFont.systemFontOfSize(12)
    let attributes = [NSFontAttributeName: font]
    let attributedText = NSAttributedString(string: text, attributes: attributes)
    attributedText.drawInRect(frame)
```

The only attribute we support is fill color. It's very easy to add support for extra attributes, but we left that out for brevity. To draw a diagram with a FillColor attribute, we save the current graphics state, set the fill color, draw the diagram, and finally, restore the graphics state:

```
case .Attributed(.FillColor(let color), let d):
    CGContextSaveGState(self)
    color.set()
    draw(bounds, d)
```

```
CGContextRestoreGState(self)
```

To draw two diagrams next to each other, we first need to find their respective frames. We extend CGRect with a function, split, that splits a CGRect according to a ratio (in this case, the relative size of the left diagram). Then we draw both diagrams with their frames:

```
case .Beside(let left, let right):
    let (lFrame, rFrame) = bounds.split(
        left.size.width/diagram.size.width, edge: .MinXEdge)
    draw(lFrame, left)
    draw(rFrame, right)
```

The split function is defined as the following:

```
extension CGRect {
    func split(ratio: CGFloat, edge: CGRectEdge) -> (CGRect, CGRect) {
        let length = edge.isHorizontal ? width : height
        return divide(length * ratio, fromEdge: edge)
    }
}

extension CGRectEdge {
    var isHorizontal: Bool {
        return self == .MaxXEdge || self == .MinXEdge;
    }
}
```

The case for Below is exactly the same, except that we split the CGRect vertically instead of horizontally. This code was written to run on the Mac, and therefore the order is bottom and top (unlike UIKit, the Cocoa coordinate system has the origin at the bottom left):

```
case .Below(let top, let bottom):
    let (lFrame, rFrame) = bounds.split(
        bottom.size.height/diagram.size.height, edge: .MinYEdge)
    draw(lFrame, bottom)
    draw(rFrame, top)
```

Our last case is aligning diagrams. Here, we can reuse the fit function that we defined earlier to calculate new bounds that fit the diagram exactly:

```
        case .Align(let vec, let diagram):
            let frame = diagram.size.fit(vec, bounds)
```

```
            draw(frame, diagram)
        }
    }
}
```

We've now defined the core of our library. All the other things can be built on top of these primitives.

Creating Views and PDFs

We can create a subclass of NSView that performs the drawing, which is very useful when working with playgrounds or when you want to draw these diagrams in Mac applications:

```
class Draw: NSView {
    let diagram: Diagram

    init(frame frameRect: NSRect, diagram: Diagram) {
        self.diagram = diagram
        super.init(frame:frameRect)
    }

    required init(coder: NSCoder) {
        fatalError("NSCoding not supported")
    }

    override func drawRect(dirtyRect: NSRect) {
        guard let context = NSGraphicsContext.currentContext() else { return }
        context.cgContext.draw(self.bounds, diagram)
    }
}
```

Now that we have an NSView, it's also very simple to make a PDF out of our diagrams. We calculate the size and just use NSView's method, dataWithPDFInsideRect, to get the PDF data. This is a nice example of taking existing object-oriented code and wrapping it in a functional layer:

```
extension Diagram {
    func pdf(width: CGFloat) -> NSData {
        let height = width * (size.height / size.width)
        let v = Draw(frame: NSMakeRect(0, 0, width, height), diagram: self)
        return v.dataWithPDFInsideRect(v.bounds)
    }
```

```
}
```

Extra Combinators

To make the construction of diagrams easier, it's nice to add some extra
functions (also called combinators). This is a common pattern in functional
libraries: have a small set of core data types and functions and then build
convenience functions on top of them. For example, for rectangles, circles,
text, and squares, we can define convenience functions like so:

```
func rect(width width: CGFloat, height: CGFloat) -> Diagram {
    return .Prim(CGSizeMake(width, height), .Rectangle)
}

func circle(diameter diameter: CGFloat) -> Diagram {
    return .Prim(CGSizeMake(diameter, diameter), .Ellipse)
}

func text(theText: String, width: CGFloat, height: CGFloat) -> Diagram {
    return .Prim(CGSizeMake(width, height), .Text(theText))
}

func square(side side: CGFloat) -> Diagram {
    return rect(width: side, height: side)
}
```

Also, it turns out that it's very convenient to have operators for combining
diagrams horizontally and vertically, making the code more readable. They are
just wrappers around Beside and Below:

```
infix operator ||| { associativity left }
func ||| (l: Diagram, r: Diagram) -> Diagram {
    return Diagram.Beside(l, r)
}

infix operator --- { associativity left }
func --- (l: Diagram, r: Diagram) -> Diagram {
    return Diagram.Below(l, r)
}
```

We can also extend the Diagram type and add methods for filling and
alignment. We also might have defined these methods as top-level functions
instead. This is a matter of style; one is not more powerful than the other:

```
extension Diagram {
    func fill (color: NSColor) -> Diagram {
        return .Attributed(.FillColor(color), self)
    }

    func alignTop() -> Diagram {
        return .Align(CGVector(dx: 0.5, dy: 1), self)
    }

    func alignBottom() -> Diagram {
        return .Align(CGVector(dx: 0.5, dy: 0), self)
    }
}
```

Finally, we can define an empty diagram and a way to horizontally concatenate a list of diagrams. We can just use the array's reduce function to do this:

```
let empty: Diagram = rect(width: 0, height: 0)

func hcat(diagrams: [Diagram]) -> Diagram {
    return diagrams.reduce(empty, combine: |||)
}
```

By adding these small helper functions, we have a powerful library for drawing diagrams.

Discussion

The code in this chapter is inspired by the Diagrams library for Haskell (Yorgey 2012). Although we can draw simple diagrams, there are many possible improvements and extensions to the library we have presented here. Some things are still missing but can be added easily. For example, it's straightforward to add more attributes and styling options. A bit more complicated would be adding transformations (such as rotation), but this is certainly still possible.

When we compare the library that we've built in this chapter to the library in Chapter 2, we can see many similarities. Both take a problem domain (regions and diagrams) and create a small library of functions to describe this domain. Both libraries provide an interface through functions that are highly composable. Both of these little libraries define a *domain-specific language* (or

DSL) embedded in Swift. A DSL is a small programming language tailored to solve a particular problem.

You are probably already familiar with lots of DSLs, such as regular expressions, SQL, or HTML — each of these languages is not a general-purpose programming language in which to write *any* application, but instead is more restricted to solve a particular kind of problem. Regular expressions are used for describing patterns or lexers, SQL is used for querying a database, and HTML is used for describing the content of a webpage.

However, there is an important difference between the two DSLs we've built in this book: in the chapter on thinking functionally, we created functions that return a boolean for each position. To draw the diagrams, we built up an intermediate structure, the Diagram enum. A *shallow embedding* of a DSL in a general-purpose programming language like Swift does not create any intermediate data structures. A *deep embedding*, on the other hand, explicitly creates an intermediate data structure, like the Diagram enumeration described in this chapter.

The term embedding refers to how the DSL for regions or diagrams are embedded into Swift. Both have their advantages. A shallow embedding can be easier to write, there is less overhead during execution, and it can be easier to extend with new functions. However, when using a deep embedding, we have the advantage of analyzing an entire structure, transforming it, or assigning different meanings to the intermediate data structure.

If we would rewrite the DSL from Chapter 2 to instead use deep embedding, we would need to define an enumeration representing the different functions from the library. There would be members for our primitive regions, like circles or squares, and members for composite regions, such as those formed by intersection or union. We could then analyze and compute with these regions in different ways: generating images, checking whether or not a region is primitive, determining whether or not a given point is in the region, or performing an arbitrary computation over the intermediate data structure.

Rewriting the diagrams library from this chapter to a shallow embedding would be complicated. The intermediate data structure can be inspected, modified, and transformed. To define a shallow embedding, we would need to call Core Graphics directly for every operation that we wish to support in our DSL. It is much more difficult to compose drawing calls than it is to first create an intermediate structure and only render it once the diagram has been completely assembled.

Generators and Sequences

In this chapter, we'll look at generators and sequences. These form the machinery underlying Swift's **for** loops and will be the basis of the parsing library that we will present in the following chapters.

Generators

In Objective-C and Swift, we almost always use the Array datatype to represent a list of items. It is both simple and fast. There are situations, however, where arrays are not suitable. For example, you might not want to calculate all the elements of an array, because there is an infinite amount, or you don't expect to use them all. In such situations, you may want to use a *generator* instead.

To get started, we will provide some motivation for generators, using familiar examples from array computations.

Swift's **for** loops can be used to iterate over array elements:

```
for x in xs {
    // do something with x
}
```

In such a **for** loop, the array is traversed from beginning to end. There may be examples, however, where you want to traverse arrays in a different order. This is where generators may be useful.

Conceptually, a generator is a 'process' that generates new array elements on request. A generator is any type that adheres to the following protocol:

```
protocol GeneratorType {
    typealias Element
    func next() -> Element?
}
```

This protocol requires an *associated type*, Element, defined by the GeneratorType. There is a single method, next, that produces the next element if it exists and **nil** otherwise.

For example, the following generator produces array indices, starting from the end of an array until it reaches 0. The Element type is derived from the next function; we do not need to specify it explicitly:

```
class CountdownGenerator: GeneratorType {
```

```
    var element: Int

    init<T>(array: [T]) {
        self.element = array.count - 1
    }

    func next() -> Int? {
        return self.element < 0 ? nil : element--
    }
}
```

We define an initializer that is passed an array and initializes the element to the array's last valid index.

We can use this CountdownGenerator to traverse an array's indices backward:

```
let xs = ["A", "B", "C"]

let generator = CountdownGenerator(array: xs)
while let i = generator.next() {
    print("Element \(i) of the array is \(xs[i])")
}

Element 2 of the array is C
Element 1 of the array is B
Element 0 of
the array is A
```

Although it may seem like overkill on such simple examples, the generator encapsulates the computation of array indices. If we want to compute the indices in a different order, we only need to update the generator and never the code that uses it.

Generators need not produce a **nil** value at some point. For example, we can define a generator that produces an 'infinite' series of powers of two (until NSDecimalNumber overflows, which is only with extremely large values):

```
class PowerGenerator: GeneratorType {
    var power: NSDecimalNumber = 1
    let two: NSDecimalNumber = 2

    func next() -> NSDecimalNumber? {
        power = power.decimalNumberByMultiplyingBy(two)
        return power
```

```
        }
}
```

We can use the PowerGenerator to inspect increasingly large array indices, for example, when implementing an exponential search algorithm that doubles the array index in every iteration.

We may also want to use the PowerGenerator for something entirely different. Suppose we want to search through the powers of two, looking for some interesting value. The findPower function takes a predicate of type NSDecimalNumber -> Bool as argument and returns the smallest power of two that satisfies this predicate:

```
extension PowerGenerator {
    func findPower(predicate: NSDecimalNumber -> Bool) -> NSDecimalNumber {
        while let x = next() {
            if predicate(x) {
                return x
            }
        }
        return 0
    }
}
```

We can use the findPower function to compute the smallest power of two larger than 1,000:

```
PowerGenerator().findPower { $0.integerValue > 1000 }
```

```
1024
```

The generators we have seen so far all produce numerical elements, but this need not be the case. We can just as well write generators that produce some other value. For example, the following generator produces a list of strings, corresponding to the lines of a file:

```
class FileLinesGenerator: GeneratorType {
    typealias Element = String

    var lines: [String] = []

    init(filename: String) throws {
        let contents: String = try String(contentsOfFile: filename)
        let newLine = NSCharacterSet.newlineCharacterSet()
```

```
        lines = contents .componentsSeparatedByCharactersInSet(newLine)
    }

    func next() -> Element? {
        guard !lines.isEmpty else { return nil }
        let  nextLine = lines.removeAtIndex(0)
        return nextLine
    }
}
```

By defining generators in this fashion, we separate the *generation* of data from its *usage*. The generation may involve opening a file or URL and handling the errors that arise. Hiding this behind a simple generator protocol helps keep the code that manipulates the generated data oblivious to these issues.

By defining a protocol for generators, we can also write generic functions that work for every generator. For instance, our previous findPower function can be generalized as follows:

```
extension GeneratorType {
    mutating func find(predicate: Element -> Bool) -> Element? {
        while let  x = self .next()  {
            if  predicate(x) {
                return x
            }
        }
        return nil
    }
}
```

The find function is now available in any possible generator. The most interesting thing about it is its type signature. The generator may be modified by the find function, resulting from the calls to next, hence we need to add the **mutating** annotation in the type declaration. The predicate should be a function mapping generated elements to Bool. We can refer to the generator's associated type as Element, in the type signature of find. Finally, note that we may not succeed in finding a value that satisfies the predicate. For that reason, find returns an optional value, returning **nil** when the generator is exhausted.

It is also possible to combine generators on top of one another. For example, you may want to limit the number of items generated, buffer the generated values, or encrypt the data generated. Here is one simple example of a generator transformer that produces the first limit values from its argument generator:

```swift
class LimitGenerator<G: GeneratorType>: GeneratorType {
    var limit = 0
    var generator: G

    init(limit: Int, generator: G) {
        self.limit = limit
        self.generator = generator
    }

    func next() -> G.Element? {
        guard limit >= 0 else { return nil }
        limit--
        return generator.next()
    }
}
```

Such a generator may be useful when populating an array of a fixed size, or somehow buffering the elements generated.

When writing generators, it can sometimes be cumbersome to introduce new classes for every generator. Swift provides a simple class, AnyGenerator<Element>, which is generic in the element type. It can be initialized with a next function:

```swift
class AnyGenerator<Element>: GeneratorType, SequenceType {
    init(next: () -> Element?)
        ...
```

We will provide the complete definition of AnyGenerator shortly. For now, we'd like to point out that the AnyGenerator struct not only implements the GeneratorType protocol, but it also implements the SequenceType protocol that we will cover in the next section.

Using AnyGenerator allows for much shorter definitions of generators. For example, we can rewrite our CountdownGenerator as follows:

```swift
extension Int {
    func countDown() -> AnyGenerator<Int> {
        var i = self
        return anyGenerator { i < 0 ? nil : i-- }
    }
}
```

We can even define functions to manipulate and combine generators in terms of AnyGenerator. For example, we can append two generators with the same underlying element type, as follows:

```
func +<G: GeneratorType, H: GeneratorType where G.Element == H.Element>
    (var first : G, var second: H) -> AnyGenerator<G.Element>
{
    return anyGenerator { first.next() ?? second.next() }
}
```

The resulting generator simply reads off new elements from its first argument generator; once this is exhausted, it produces elements from its second generator. Once both generators have returned nil, the composite generator also returns nil.

Sequences

Generators form the basis of another Swift protocol, *sequences*. Generators provide a 'one-shot' mechanism for repeatedly computing a next element. There is no way to rewind or replay the elements generated. The only thing we can do is create a fresh generator and use that instead. The SequenceType protocol provides just the right interface for doing that:

```
protocol SequenceType {
    typealias Generator: GeneratorType
    func generate() -> Generator
}
```

Every sequence has an associated generator type and a method to create a new generator. We can then use this generator to traverse the sequence. For example, we can use our CountdownGenerator to define a sequence that generates a series of array indexes in back-to-front order:

```
struct ReverseSequence<T>: SequenceType {
    var array: [T]

    init (array: [T]) {
        self.array = array
    }

    func generate() -> CountdownGenerator {
        return CountdownGenerator(array: array)
```

```
        }
}
```

Every time we want to traverse the array stored in the ReverseSequence struct, we can call the generate method to produce the desired generator. The following example shows how to fit these pieces together:

```
let reverseSequence = ReverseSequence(array: xs)
let reverseGenerator = reverseSequence.generate()

while let i = reverseGenerator.next() {
    print("Index \(i) is \(xs[i])")
}
```

```
Index 2 is C
Index 1 is B
Index 0 is A
```

In contrast to the previous example that just used the generator, the *same* sequence can be traversed a second time — we would simply call generate to produce a new generator. By encapsulating the creation of generators in the SequenceType definition, programmers using sequences do not have to be concerned with the creation of the underlying generators. This is in line with the object-oriented philosophy of separating use and creation, which tends to result in more cohesive code.

Swift has special syntax for working with sequences. Instead of creating the generator associated with a sequence yourself, you can write a for-in loop. For example, we can also write the previous code snippet as the following:

```
for i in ReverseSequence(array: xs) {
    print("Index \(i) is \(xs[i])")
}
```

```
Index 2 is C
Index 1 is B
Index 0 is A
```

Under the hood, Swift then uses the generate method to produce a generator and repeatedly calls its next function until it produces **nil**.

The obvious drawback of our CountdownGenerator is that it produces numbers, while we may be interested in the *elements* associated with an array.

Fortunately, there are standard map and filter functions that manipulate sequences rather than arrays:

```
public protocol SequenceType {
    public func map<T>(
        @noescape transform: (Self.Generator.Element) throws -> T)
        rethrows -> [T]

    public func filter (
        @noescape includeElement: (Self.Generator.Element) throws -> Bool)
        rethrows -> [Self.Generator.Element]
}
```

To produce the *elements* of an array in reverse order, we can map over our ReverseSequence:

```
let reverseElements = ReverseSequence(array: xs).map { xs[$0] }
for x in reverseElements {
    print("Element is \(x)")
}
```

```
Element is C
Element is B
Element is A
```

Similarly, we may of course want to filter out certain elements from a sequence.

It is worth pointing out that these map and filter functions do *not* return new sequences, but instead traverse the sequence to produce an array. Mathematicians may therefore object to calling such operations maps, as they fail to leave the underlying structure (a sequence) intact. There are separate versions of map and filter that do produce sequences. These are defined as extensions of the LazySequence class. A LazySequence is a simple wrapper around regular sequences and can be obtained via a sequence's **lazy** property:

```
extension SequenceType {
    public var lazy: LazySequence<Self> { get }
}
```

If you need to map or filter sequences that may produce either infinite results, or many results that you may not be interested in, be sure to use a LazySequence rather than a Sequence. Failing to do so could cause your program to diverge or take much longer than you might expect.

Case Study: Traversing a Binary Tree

To illustrate sequences and generators, we will consider defining a traversal on a binary tree. Recall our definition of binary trees from Chapter 9:

```
indirect enum BinarySearchTree<Element: Comparable> {
    case Leaf
    case Node(BinarySearchTree<Element>, Element, BinarySearchTree<Element>)
}
```

Before we define a generator that produces the elements of this tree, we need to define an auxiliary function. In the Swift standard library, there is a GeneratorOfOne struct that can be useful for wrapping an optional value as a generator:

```
struct GeneratorOfOne<Element>: GeneratorType, SequenceType {
    init (_ element: Element?)
    // ...
}
```

Given an optional element, it generates the sequence with just that element (provided it is non-**nil**):

```
let three: [Int] = Array(GeneratorOfOne(3))
let empty: [Int] = Array(GeneratorOfOne(nil))
```

For the sake of convenience, we will define our own little wrapper function around GeneratorOfOne:

```
func one<T>(x: T?) -> AnyGenerator<T> {
    return anyGenerator(GeneratorOfOne(x))
}
```

We can use this one function, together with the append operator on generators, +, to produce sequences of elements of a binary tree. For example, the inOrder traversal visits the left subtree, the root, and the right subtree, in that order:

```
extension BinarySearchTree {
    var inOrder: AnyGenerator<Element> {
        switch self {
        case .Leaf:
            return anyGenerator { return nil }
        case .Node(let left, let x, let right):
```

```
        return left.inOrder + one(x) + right.inOrder
    }
  }
}
```

If the tree has no elements, we return an empty generator. If the tree has a node, we combine the results of the two recursive calls, together with the single value stored at the root, using the append operator on generators.

Case Study: Better Shrinking in QuickCheck

In this section, we will provide a somewhat larger case study of defining sequences, by improving the Smaller protocol we implemented in the QuickCheck chapter. Originally, the protocol was defined as follows:

```
protocol Smaller {
    func smaller() -> Self?
}
```

We used the Smaller protocol to try and shrink counterexamples that our testing uncovered. The smaller function is repeatedly called to generate a smaller value; if this value still fails the test, it is considered a 'better' counterexample than the original one. The Smaller instance we defined for arrays simply tried to repeatedly strip off the first element:

```
extension Array: Smaller {
    func smaller() -> [T]? {
        guard !self.isEmpty else { return nil }
        return Array(dropFirst())
    }
}
```

While this will certainly help shrink counterexamples in *some* cases, there are many different ways to shrink an array. Computing all possible subarrays is an expensive operation. For an array of length n, there are 2^n possible subarrays that may or may not be interesting counterexamples — generating and testing them is not a good idea.

Instead, we will show how to use a generator to produce a series of smaller values. We can then adapt our QuickCheck library to use the following protocol:

```
protocol Smaller {
    func smaller() -> AnyGenerator<Self>
}
```

When QuickCheck finds a counterexample, we can then rerun our tests on the series of smaller values until we have found a suitably small counterexample. The only thing we still have to do is write a smaller function for arrays (and any other type that we might want to shrink).

As a first step, instead of removing just the first element of the array, we will compute a series of arrays, where each new array has one element removed. This will not produce all possible sublists, but only a sequence of arrays in which each array is one element shorter than the original array. Using AnyGenerator, we can define such a function as follows:

```
extension Array {
    func generateSmallerByOne() -> AnyGenerator<[Element]> {
        var i = 0
        return anyGenerator {
            guard i < self.count else { return nil }
            var result = self
            result.removeAtIndex(i)
            i++
            return result
        }
    }
}
```

The generateSmallerByOne function keeps track of a variable i. When asked for the next element, it checks whether or not i is less than the length of the array. If so, it computes a new array, result, and increments i. If we have reached the end of our original array, we return nil.

We can now see that this returns all possible arrays that are one element smaller:

```
[1, 2, 3].generateSmallerByOne()
```

Unfortunately, this call does not produce the desired result — it defines an AnyGenerator<[Int]>, whereas we would like to see an array of arrays.

Fortunately, there is an Array initializer that takes a Sequence as argument. Using that initializer, we can test our generator as follows:

```
Array([1, 2, 3].generateSmallerByOne())
```

```
[[2, 3], [1, 3], [1, 2]]
```

Using the decompose function, we can redefine the smaller function on arrays. If we try to formulate a recursive pseudocode definition of what our original generateSmallerByOne function computed, we might arrive at something along the following lines:

→ If the array is empty, return **nil**

→ If the array can be split into a head and tail, we can recursively compute the remaining subarrays as follows:

→ tail of the array is a subarray

→ if we prepend head to all the subarrays of the tail, we can compute the subarrays of the original array

We can translate this algorithm directly into Swift with the functions we have defined:

```
extension Array {
    func smaller1() -> AnyGenerator<[Element]> {
        guard let (head, tail) = self.decompose else { return one(nil) }
        return one(tail) + Array<[Element]>(tail.smaller1()).map { smallerTail in
            [head] + smallerTail
        }.generate()
    }
}
```

We're now ready to test our functional variant, and we can verify that it's the same result as generateSmallerByOne:

```
Array([1, 2, 3].smaller1())
```

```
[[2, 3], [1, 3], [1, 2]]
```

There is one last improvement worth making: there is one more way to try and reduce the counterexamples that QuickCheck finds. Instead of just removing elements, we may also want to try and shrink the elements themselves. To do that, we need to add a condition that T conforms to the smaller protocol:

```
extension Array where Element: Smaller {
    func smaller() -> AnyGenerator<[Element]> {
        guard let (head, tail) = self.decompose else { return one(nil) }
        let gen1 = one(tail).generate()
        let gen2 = Array<[Element]>(tail.smaller()).map { xs in
            [head] + xs
        }.generate()
        let gen3 = Array<Element>(head.smaller()).map { x in
            [x] + tail
        }.generate()
        return gen1 + gen2 + gen3
    }
}
```

We can check the results of our new smaller function:

```
Array([1, 2, 3].smaller())
```

```
[[2, 3], [1, 3], [1, 2], [1, 2, 2], [1, 1, 3], [0, 2, 3]]
```

In addition to generating sublists, this new version of the smaller function also produces arrays, where the values of the elements are smaller.

Beyond Map and Filter

In the coming chapter, we will need a few more operations on sequences and generators. To define those operations, we need the AnySequence struct, defined analogously to the AnyGenerator we saw previously. Essentially, it wraps any function that returns a generator in a sequence. It is (more or less) defined as follows:

```
struct AnySequence<Element>: SequenceType {
    init<G: GeneratorType where G.Element == Element>
        (_ makeUnderlyingGenerator: () -> G)

    func generate() -> AnyGenerator<Element>
}
```

We have already defined concatenation, using the + operator, on generators. A first attempt at defining concatenation for sequences might result in the following definition:

```
func +<A>(l: AnySequence<A>, r: AnySequence<A>) -> AnySequence<A> {
```

```
    return AnySequence(l.generate() + r.generate())
}
```

This definition calls the generate method of the two argument sequences, concatenates these, and assigns the resulting generator to the sequence. Unfortunately, it does not quite work as expected. Consider the following example:

```
let s = AnySequence([1, 2, 3]) + AnySequence([4, 5, 6])
print("First pass: ")
for x in s {
    print(x)
}
print("Second pass:")
for x in s {
    print(x)
}
```

We construct a sequence containing the elements [1, 2, 3, 4, 5, 6] and traverse it twice, printing the elements we encounter. Somewhat surprisingly perhaps, this code produces the following output:

```
First pass: 123456
Second pass:
```

The second **for** loop is not producing any output — what went wrong? The problem is in the definition of concatenation on sequences. We assemble the desired generator, l.generate() + r.generate(). This generator produces all the desired elements in the first loop in the example above. Once it has been exhausted, however, traversing the compound sequence a second time will not produce a fresh generator, but instead use the generator that has already been exhausted.

Fortunately, this problem is easy to fix. We need to ensure that the result of our concatenation operation can produce new generators. To do so, we pass a *function* that produces generators, rather than passing a fixed generator to the AnySequence initializer:

```
func +<A>(l: AnySequence<A>, r: AnySequence<A>) -> AnySequence<A> {
    return AnySequence { l.generate() + r.generate() }
}
```

Now, we can iterate over the same sequence multiple times. When writing your own methods that combine sequences, it is important to ensure that every call to generate() produces a fresh generator that is oblivious to any previous traversals.

Thus far, we can concatenate two sequences. What about flattening a sequence of sequences? Before we deal with sequences, let's try writing a join operation that, given an AnyGenerator<AnyGenerator<A>>, produces an AnyGenerator<A>:

```
struct JoinedGenerator<Element>: GeneratorType {
    var generator: AnyGenerator<AnyGenerator<Element>>
    var current: AnyGenerator<Element>?

    init<G: GeneratorType where G.Element: GeneratorType,
        G.Element.Element == Element>(var _ g: G)
    {
        generator = g.map(anyGenerator)
        current = generator.next()
    }

    mutating func next() -> Element? {
        guard let c = current else { return nil }
        if let x = c.next() {
            return x
        } else {
            current = generator.next()
            return next()
        }
    }
}
```

This JoinedGenerator maintains two pieces of mutable state: an optional current generator, and the remaining generators. When asked to produce the next element, it calls the next function on the current generator, if it exists. When this fails, it updates the current generator and *recursively* calls next again. Only when all the generators have been exhausted does the next function return **nil**.

Next, we use this JoinedGenerator to join a sequence of sequences:

```
extension SequenceType where Generator.Element: SequenceType {
    typealias NestedElement = Generator.Element.Generator.Element

    func join() -> AnySequence<NestedElement> {
        return AnySequence { () -> JoinedGenerator<NestedElement> in
            var generator = self.generate()
```

```
            return JoinedGenerator(generator.map { $0.generate() })
        }
    }
}
```

First we define a type alias, NestedElement, for the type of the nested
sequences' elements. The return type then becomes
AnySequence<NestedElement>. We create such an instance by initializing
AnySequence with a function that returns a JoinedGenerator<NestedElement>.
To create the nested generators, we call generate() on **self**, which gives us a
value of type AnyGenerator<AnySequence<A>>. All that's left to do is to map
over those sequences and call generate() on each of them, which is precisely
what the call to map accomplishes.

Finally, we can also combine join and map to write the following flatMap
function:

```
extension AnySequence {
    func flatMap<T, Seq: SequenceType where Seq.Generator.Element == T>
        (f: Element -> Seq) -> AnySequence<T>
    {
        return AnySequence<Seq>(self.map(f)).join()
    }
}
```

Given a sequence with elements of type Element, and a function f that, given a
single value of type Element, produces a new sequence of T elements, we can
build a single sequence of T elements. To do so, we simply map f over the
argument sequence, constructing an AnySequence<AnySequence<T>>, which
we join to obtain the desired AnySequence<T>.

Now that we've got a good grip on sequences and the operations they support,
we can proceed to our next case study: writing a parser combinator library.

Case Study: Parser Combinators

12

Parsers are very useful tools: they take a list of tokens (usually, a list of characters) and transform it into a structure. Often, parsers are generated using an external tool, such as Bison or YACC. Instead of using an external tool in, in this chapter we'll build a parser library, which we can use later for building our own parser. Functional languages are very well suited for this task.

There are several approaches to writing a parsing library. Here we'll build a parser combinator library. A parser combinator is a higher-order function that takes several parsers as input and returns a new parser as its output. The library we'll build is an almost direct port of a Haskell library (2009), with a few modifications.

We will start with defining a couple of core combinators. On top of that, we will build some extra convenience functions, and finally, we will show an example that parses arithmetic expressions — such as 1+3*3 — and calculates the result.

The Core

In this library, we'll make heavy use of sequences and slices.

We define a parser as a function that takes a slice of tokens, processes some of these tokens, and returns a tuple of the result and the remainder of the tokens. To make our lives a bit easier, we wrap this function in a struct (otherwise, we'd have to write out the entire type every time). We make our parser generic over two types, Token and Result:

```
struct Parser<Token, Result> {
    let p: ArraySlice<Token> -> AnySequence<(Result, ArraySlice<Token>)>
}
```

We'd rather use a type alias to define our parser type, but type aliases don't support generic types. Therefore, we have to live with the indirection of using a struct in this case.

Let's start with a very simple parser that parses the single character "a". To do this, we write a function that returns the "a" character parser:

```
func parseA() -> Parser<Character, Character>
```

To return this single result, we use the one function, which constructs a sequence with one element, defined analogously to the function one returning a Generator in the previous chapter:

```
func one<A>(x: A) -> AnySequence<A> {
    return AnySequence(GeneratorOfOne(x))
}
```

If the first character isn't an "a", the parser fails by returning **none**(), which is simply an empty sequence. The complete parseA function looks like this:

```
func parseA() -> Parser<Character, Character> {
    let a: Character = "a"
    return Parser { x in
        guard let (head, tail) = x.decompose where head == a else {
            return none()
        }
        return one((a, tail ))
    }
}
```

We test the parser using a function called testParser:

```
func testParser<A>(parser: Parser<Character, A>, _ input: String) -> String {
    var result: [String] = []
    for (x, s) in parser.p(input.slice) {
        result += ["Success, found \(x), remainder: \(Array(s))"]
    }
    return result.isEmpty ? "Parsing failed." : result.joinWithSeparator("\n")
}
```

This runs the parser given by the first argument over the input string that is given by the second argument. The parser will generate a sequence of possible results, which get printed out by the testParser function:

```
testParser(parseA(), "abcd")
```

```
Success, found a, remainder: ["b", "c", "d"]
```

If we run the parser on a string that doesn't contain an "a" at the start, we get a failure:

```
testParser(parseA(), "test")
```

Parsing failed.

We can easily abstract the parseA function to work on any character. We pass
in the character we want it to parse as a parameter, and we only return a result
if the first character in the stream is the same as the parameter:

```
func parseCharacter(character: Character) -> Parser<Character, Character> {
    return Parser { x in
        guard let (head, tail) = x.decompose where head == character else {
            return none()
        }
        return one((character, tail))
    }
}
```

We can use parseCharacter like this:

```
testParser(parseCharacter("t"), "test")
```

```
Success, found t, remainder: ["e", "s", "t"]
```

We can abstract this method one final time, making it generic over any kind of
token. Instead of checking if the token is equal, we pass in a function with type
Token -> Bool, and if the function returns true for the first character in the
stream, we return it:

```
func satisfy<Token>(condition: Token -> Bool) -> Parser<Token, Token> {
    return Parser { x in
        guard let (head, tail) = x.decompose where condition(head) else {
            return none()
        }
        return one((head, tail))
    }
}
```

Now we can define a function token that works like parseCharacter, the only
difference being that it can be used with any type that conforms to Equatable:

```
func token<Token: Equatable>(t: Token) -> Parser<Token, Token> {
    return satisfy { $0 == t }
}
```

Choice

Parsing a single symbol isn't very useful, unless we add functions to combine two parsers. The first function that we will introduce is the choice operator: <|>. It can parse using either the left operand or the right operand.

The choice operator is implemented in a simple way: given an input string, it runs the left operand's parser, which yields a sequence of possible results. Then it runs the right operand, which also yields a sequence of possible results, and it concatenates the two sequences. Note that the left and the right sequences might both be empty, or they might contain a lot of elements. But because they are calculated lazily, it doesn't really matter:

```
infix operator <|> { associativity right precedence 130 }
func <|> <Token, A>(l: Parser<Token, A>, r: Parser<Token, A>)
    -> Parser<Token, A>
{
    return Parser { l.p($0) + r.p($0) }
}
```

To test our new operator, we build a parser that parses either an "a" or a "b":

```
let a: Character = "a"
let b: Character = "b"

testParser(token(a) <|> token(b), "bcd")

Success, found b, remainder: ["c", "d"]
```

Sequence

To combine two parsers that occur after each other, we'll start with a more naive approach and expand that later to something more convenient and powerful. First we write a sequence function:

```
func sequence<Token, A, B>(l: Parser<Token, A>, _ r: Parser<Token, B>)
    -> Parser<Token, (A, B)>
```

The retuned parser first uses the left parser to parse something of type A. Let's say we wanted to parse the string "xyz" for an "x" immediately followed by a "y." The left parser (the one looking for an "x") would then generate the following sequence containing a single (result, remainder) tuple:

```
[ ("x", "yz") ]
```

Applying the right parser to the remainder ("yz") of the left parser's tuple yields another sequence with one tuple:

```
[ ("y", "z") ]
```

We then combine those tuples by grouping the "x" and "y" into a new tuple ("x", "y"):

```
[ (("x", "y"), "z") ]
```

Since we are doing these steps for each tuple in the returned sequence of the left parser, we end up with a sequence of sequences:

```
[ [ (("x", "y"), "z") ] ]
```

Finally, we flatten this structure to a simple sequence of ((A, B), ArraySlice<Token>) tuples. In code, the whole sequence function looks like this:

```
func sequence<Token, A, B>(l: Parser<Token, A>, _ r: Parser<Token, B>)
    -> Parser<Token, (A, B)>
{
    return Parser { input in
        let leftResults = l.p(input)
        return leftResults.flatMap {
            (a, leftRest) -> [((A, B), ArraySlice<Token>)] in
            let rightResults = r.p(leftRest)
            return rightResults.map { b, rightRest in
                ((a, b), rightRest)
            }
        }
    }
}
```

We can test our parser by trying to parse a sequence of an "x" followed by a "y":

```
let x: Character = "x"
let y: Character = "y"
```

```
let p: Parser<Character, (Character, Character)> = sequence(token(x), token(y))
testParser(p, "xyz")
```

Success, found ("x", "y"), remainder: ["z"]

Refining Sequences

The sequence function we wrote above is a first approach to combine multiple
parsers that are applied after each other. Imagine we wanted to parse the same
string "xyz" as above, but this time we want to parse "x", followed by "y",
followed by "z". We could try to use the sequence function in a nested way to
combine three parsers:

```
let z: Character = "z"
```

```
let p2 = sequence(sequence(token(x), token(y)), token(z))
testParser(p2, "xyz")
```

Success, found (("x", "y"), "z"), remainder: []

The problem of this approach is that it yields a nested tuple (("x", "y"), "z")
instead of a flat one ("x", "y", "z"). To rectify this, we could write a sequence3
function by simply extending the sequence function above, which combines
three parsers instead of just two:

```
func sequence3<Token, A, B, C>(p1: Parser<Token, A>, _ p2: Parser<Token, B>,
    _ p3: Parser<Token, C>) -> Parser<Token, (A, B, C)>
{
    typealias Result = ((A, B, C), ArraySlice<Token>)
    typealias Results = [Result]

    return Parser { input in
        let p1Results = p1.p(input)
        return p1Results.flatMap { a, p1Rest -> Results in
            let p2Results = p2.p(p1Rest)
            return p2Results.flatMap {b, p2Rest -> Results in
                let p3Results = p3.p(p2Rest)
                return p3Results.map { (c, p3Rest) -> Result in
                    ((a, b, c),  p3Rest)
                }
            }
        }
    }
}
```

```
let p3 = sequence3(token(x), token(y), token(z))
testParser(p3, "xyz")
```

```
Success, found ("x", "y", "z"),  remainder: []
```

This returns the expected result, but the approach is way too inflexible and doesn't scale. It turns out there is a much more convenient way to combine multiple parsers in sequence.

As a first step, we create a parser that consumes no tokens at all and returns a function, A -> B. This function takes on the job of transforming the result of one or more other parsers in the way we want it to. A very simple example of such a parser could be the following:

```
func integerParser<Token>() -> Parser<Token, Character -> Int> {
    return Parser { input in
        return one(({ x in Int(String(x))! }, input))
    }
}
```

This parser doesn't consume any tokens and returns a function that takes a character and turns it into an integer. Let's use the extremely simple input stream "3" as example. Applying the integerParser to this input yields the following sequence:

```
[ (A -> B, "3") ]
```

Applying another parser to parse the symbol "3" in the remainder (which is equal to the original input since the integerParser didn't consume any tokens) yields:

```
[ ("3", "") ]
```

Now we just have to create a function that combines these two parsers and returns a new parser, so that the function yielded by integerParser gets applied to the character "3" yielded by the symbol parser. This function looks very similar to the sequence function — it calls flatMap on the sequence returned by the first parser and then maps over the sequence returned by the second parser applied to the remainder.

The key difference is that the inner closure does not return the results of both parsers in a tuple as sequence did, but it applies the function yielded by the first parser to the result of the second parser:

```
func combinator<Token, A, B>(l: Parser<Token, A -> B>, _ r: Parser<Token, A>)
    -> Parser<Token, B>
{
    typealias Result = (B, ArraySlice<Token>)
    typealias Results = [Result]
    return Parser { input in
        let leftResults = l.p(input)
        return leftResults.flatMap { f, leftRemainder -> Results in
            let rightResults = r.p(leftRemainder)
            return rightResults.map { x, rightRemainder -> Result in
                (f(x), rightRemainder)
            }
        }
    }
}
```

Putting all of this together:

```
let three: Character = "3"
```

```
testParser(combinator(integerParser(), token(three)), "3")
```

```
Success, found 3, remainder: []
```

Now we've laid the groundwork to build a really elegant parser combination mechanism.

The first thing we'll do is refactor our integerParser function into a generic function, with one parameter that returns a parser that always succeeds, consumes no tokens, and returns the parameter we passed into the function as result:

```
func pure<Token, A>(value: A) -> Parser<Token, A> {
    return Parser { one((value, $0)) }
}
```

With this in place, we can rewrite the previous example like so:

```
func toInteger(c: Character) -> Int {
    return Int(String(c))!
```

```
}
testParser(combinator(pure(toInteger), token(three)), "3")
```

Success, found 3, remainder: []

The whole trick to leverage this mechanism to combine multiple parsers lies in the concept of currying. Returning a curried function from the first parser enables us to go through the combination process multiple times, depending on the number of arguments of the curried function. For example:

```
func toInteger2(c1: Character)(c2: Character) -> Int {
    let combined = String(c1) + String(c2)
    return Int(combined)!
}
```

```
testParser(combinator(combinator(pure(toInteger2), token(three)),
    token(three)), "33")
```

Success, found 33, remainder: []

Since nesting a lot of combinator calls within each other is not very readable, we define an operator for it:

```
infix operator <*> { associativity left precedence 150 }
func <*><Token, A, B>(l: Parser<Token, A -> B>, r: Parser<Token, A>)
    -> Parser<Token, B>
{
    typealias Result = (B, ArraySlice<Token>)
    typealias Results = [Result]
    return Parser { input In
        let leftResults = l.p(input)
        return leftResults.flatMap { (f, leftRemainder) -> Results in
            let rightResults = r.p(leftRemainder)
            return rightResults.map { (x, y) -> Result in (f(x), y) }
        }
    }
}
```

Now we can express the previous example as the following:

```
testParser(pure(toInteger2) <*> token(three) <*> token(three), "33")
```

Success, found 33, remainder: []

Notice that we have defined the <*> operator to have left precedence. This means that the operator will first be applied to the left two parsers and then to the result of this operation and the right parser. In other words, this behavior is exactly the same as our nested combinator function calls above.

Another example of how we can now use this operator is to create a parser that combines several characters into a string:

```
let aOrB = token(a) <|> token(b)

func combine(a: Character)(b: Character)(c: Character) -> String {
    return String([a, b, c])
}
let parser = pure(combine) <*> aOrB <*> aOrB <*> token(b)
testParser(parser, "abb")

Success, found abb, remainder: []
```

In Chapter 3, we defined the curry function, which curries a function with two parameters. We can define multiple versions of the curry function, which work on functions with different numbers of parameters. For example, we could define a variant that works on a function with three arguments, so that we can write the above parser in an even shorter way:

```
let parser2 = pure(curry { String([$0, $1, $2]) })
    <*> aOrB <*> aOrB <*> token(b)
testParser(parser2, "abb")

Success, found abb, remainder: []
```

Convenience Combinators

Using the above combinators, we can already parse a lot of interesting languages. However, they can be a bit tedious to express. Luckily, there are some extra functions we can define to make life easier. First we will define a function to parse a character from an NSCharacterSet. This can be used, for example, to create a parser that parses decimal digits:

```
func characterFromSet(set: NSCharacterSet) -> Parser<Character, Character> {
    return satisfy(set.member)
}
```

```
let decimals = NSCharacterSet.decimalDigitCharacterSet()
let decimalDigit = characterFromSet(decimals)
```

To verify that our decimalDigit parser works, we can run it on an example input string:

```
testParser(decimalDigit, "012")
```

```
Success, found 0, remainder: ["1", "2"]
```

The next convenience combinator we want to write is a zeroOrMore function, which executes a parser zero or more times:

```
func zeroOrMore<Token, A>(p: Parser<Token, A>) -> Parser<Token, [A]> {
    return (pure(prepend) <*> p <*> zeroOrMore(p)) <|> pure([])
}
```

The prepend function combines a value of type A and an array [A] into a new array:

```
func prepend<A>(l: A)(r: [A]) -> [A] {
    return [l] + r
}
```

However, if we try to use the zeroOrMore function, we will get stuck in an infinite loop. That's because of the recursive call of zeroOrMore in the return statement.

Luckily, we can use functions to defer the evaluation of the recursive call to zeroOrMore until it is really needed, and with that, break the infinite recursion. To do that, we will first define a helper function, **lazy.** It returns a parser that will only be executed once it's actually needed:

```
func lazy<Token, A>(f: () -> Parser<Token, A>) -> Parser<Token, A> {
    return Parser { f().p($0) }
}
```

Now we wrap the recursive call to zeroOrMore with this function:

```
func zeroOrMore<Token, A>(p: Parser<Token, A>) -> Parser<Token, [A]> {
    return (pure(prepend) <*> p <*> lazy { zeroOrMore(p) }) <|> pure([])
}
```

Let's test the zeroOrMore combinator to see if it yields multiple results. As we will see later on in this chapter, we usually only use the first successful result of a parser, and the other ones will never get computed, since they are lazily evaluated:

```
testParser(zeroOrMore(decimalDigit), "12345")
```

```
Success, found ["1", "2", "3", "4", "5"], remainder: []
Success,
found ["1", "2", "3", "4"], remainder: ["5"]
Success, found ["1", "2",
"3"], remainder: ["4", "5"]
Success, found ["1", "2"], remainder:
["3", "4", "5"]
Success, found ["1"], remainder: ["2", "3", "4",
"5"]
Success, found [], remainder: ["1", "2", "3", "4", "5"]
```

Another useful combinator is oneOrMore, which parses something one or more times. It is defined using the zeroOrMore combinator:

```
func oneOrMore<Token, A>(p: Parser<Token, A>) -> Parser<Token, [A]> {
    return pure(prepend) <*> p <*> zeroOrMore(p)
}
```

If we parse one or more digits, we get back an array of digits in the form of Characters. To convert this into an integer, we can first convert the array of Characters into a string and then just construct an Int out of it. Even though Int's initializer is marked as optional, we know that it will succeed, so we can force it with the ! operator:

```
let  number = pure { Int(String($0))! } <*> oneOrMore(decimalDigit)
```

```
testParser(number, "205")
```

```
Success, found 205, remainder: []
Success, found 20, remainder:
["5"]
Success, found 2, remainder: ["0", "5"]
```

Looking at the code we've written so far, we see one recurring pattern:

```
pure(x) <*> y
```

In fact, it is so common that it's useful to define an extra operator for it. If we look at the type, we can see that it's very similar to a map function — it takes a function of type A -> B and a parser of type A and returns a parser of type B:

```
infix operator </> { precedence 170 }
func </> <Token, A, B>(l: A -> B, r: Parser<Token, A>) -> Parser<Token, B> {
    return pure(l) <*> r
}
```

Now we have defined a lot of useful functions, so it's time to start combining some of them into real parsers. For example, if we want to create a parser that can add two integers, we can write it in the following way:

```
let plus: Character = "+"
func add(x: Int)(_: Character)(y: Int) -> Int {
    return x + y
}
let parseAddition = add </> number <*> token(plus) <*> number
```

And we can again verify that it works:

```
testParser(parseAddition, "41+1")
```

```
Success, found 42, remainder: []
```

It is often the case that we want to parse something but ignore the result, for example, with the plus symbol in the parser above. We want to know that it's there, but we do not care about the result of the parser. We can define another operator, <*, which works exactly like the <*> operator, except that it throws away the right-hand result after parsing it (that's why the right angular bracket is missing in the operator name). Similarly, we will also define a *> operator that throws away the left-hand result:

```
infix operator <* { associativity left precedence 150 }
func <* <Token, A, B>(p: Parser<Token, A>, q: Parser<Token, B>)
    -> Parser<Token, A>
{
    return { x in { _ in x } } </> p <*> q
}
```

```
infix operator *> { associativity left precedence 150 }
func *> <Token, A, B>(p: Parser<Token, A>, q: Parser<Token, B>)
    -> Parser<Token, B>
{
```

```
    return { _ in { y in y } } </> p <*> q
}
```

Let's write another parser for multiplication. It's very similar to the parseAddition function, except that it uses our new <* operator to throw away the "*" after parsing it:

```
let multiply: Character = "*"
let parseMultiplication = curry(*) </> number <* token(multiply) <*> number
testParser(parseMultiplication, "8*8")
```

Success, found 64, remainder: []

A Simple Calculator

We can extend our example to parse expressions like 10+4*3. Here, it is important to realize that when calculating the result, multiplication takes precedence over addition. This is because of a rule in mathematics (and programming) that's called *order of operations*. Expressing this in our parser is quite natural. Let's start with the atoms, which take the highest precedence:

```
typealias Calculator = Parser<Character, Int>

func operator0(character: Character,
               _ evaluate: (Int, Int) -> Int,
               _ operand: Calculator) -> Calculator
{
    return curry { evaluate($0, $1) } </> operand <* token(character) <*> operand
}

func pAtom0() -> Calculator { return number }
func pMultiply0() -> Calculator { return operator0("*", *, pAtom0()) }
func pAdd0() -> Calculator { return operator0("+", +, pMultiply0()) }
func pExpression0() -> Calculator { return pAdd0() }

testParser(pExpression0(), "1+3*3")
```

Parsing failed.

Why did the parsing fail?

First, an add expression is parsed. An add expression consists of a multiplication expression, followed by a "+", and then another multiplication expression. 3*3 is a multiplication expression, however, 1 is not. It's just a number. To fix this, we can change our **operator** function to parse either an expression of the form operand **operator** operand, or expressions consisting of a single operand:

```
func operator1(character: Character, _ evaluate: (Int, Int) -> Int,
    _ operand: Calculator) -> Calculator
{
    let withOperator = curry { evaluate($0, $1) } </> operand
        <* token(character) <*> operand
    return withOperator <|> operand
}
```

Now, we finally have a working variant:

```
func pAtom1() -> Calculator { return number }
func pMultiply1() -> Calculator { return operator1("*", *, pAtom1()) }
func pAdd1() -> Calculator { return operator1("+", +, pMultiply1()) }
func pExpression1() -> Calculator { return pAdd1() }

testParser(pExpression1(), "1+3*3")

Success, found 10, remainder: []
Success, found 4, remainder: ["*",
"3"]
Success, found 1, remainder: ["+", "3", "*", "3"]
```

If we want to add some more operators and abstract this a bit further, we can create an array of operator characters and their interpretation functions and use the reduce function to combine them into one parser:

```
typealias Op = (Character, (Int, Int) -> Int)
let operatorTable: [Op] = [("*", *), ("/", /), ("+", +), ("-", -)]

func pExpression2() -> Calculator {
    return operatorTable.reduce(number) { (next: Calculator, op: Op) in
        operator1(op.0, op.1, next)
    }
}

testParser(pExpression2(), "1+3*3")

Success, found 10, remainder: []
Success, found 4, remainder: ["*",
"3"]
```

Success, found 1, remainder: ["+", "3", "*", "3"]

However, our parser becomes notably slow as we add more and more operators. This is because the parser is constantly *backtracking*: it tries to parse something, then fails and tries another alternative. For example, when trying to parse "1+3*3", first, the "-" operator (which consists of a "+" expression, followed by a "-" character, and then another "+" expression) is tried. The first "+" expression succeeds, but because no "-" character is found, it tries the alternative: just a "+" expression. If we continue this, we can see that a lot of unnecessary work is being done.

Writing a parser like the above is very simple. However, it is not very efficient. If we take a step back and look at the grammar we've defined using our parser combinators, we could write it down like this (in a pseudo-grammar description language):

```
expression = min
min = add "-" add | add
add = div "+" div  |  div
div  = mul "/" mul |  mul
mul = num "*" num | num
```

To remove a lot of the duplication, we can refactor the grammar like this:

```
expression = min
min = add ("-" add)?
add = div ("+" div)?
div  = mul ("/"  mul)?
mul = num ("*" num)?
```

Before we define the new operator function, we first define an additional variant of the </> operator that consumes but doesn't use its right operand:

```
infix operator </  { precedence 170 }
func </ <Token, A, B>(l: A, r: Parser<Token, B>) -> Parser<Token, A> {
    return pure(l) <* r
}
```

Also, we will define a function, optionallyFollowed, which parses its left operand, optionally followed by another part:

```
func optionallyFollowed<A>(l: Parser<Character, A>,
    _ r: Parser<Character, A -> A>) -> Parser<Character, A>
{
```

```
let apply: A -> (A -> A) -> A = { x in { f in f(x) } }
return apply </> l <*> (r <|> pure { $0 })
}
```

Finally, we can define our operator function. It works by parsing the operand calculator, optionally followed by the operator and another operand call. Note that instead of applying evaluate, we have to flip it first (which swaps the order of the parameters). For some operators, this isn't necessary (a + b is the same as b + a), but for others, it's essential (a - b is not the same as b - a, unless b is zero):

```
func op(character: Character, _ evaluate: (Int, Int) -> Int,
    _ operand: Calculator) -> Calculator
{
    let withOperator = curry(flip(evaluate)) </ token(character) <*> operand
    return optionallyFollowed(operand, withOperator)
}
```

The flip function is defined like this:

```
func flip<A, B, C>(f: (B, A) -> C) -> (A, B) -> C {
    return { (x, y) in f(y, x) }
}
```

We now have all the ingredients to once again define our complete parser, but this time in a more efficient manner:

```
func pExpression() -> Calculator {
    return operatorTable.reduce(number) { next, inOp in
        op(inOp.0, inOp.1, next)
    }
}
```

```
testParser(pExpression() <* eof(), "10-3*2")
```

```
Success, found 4, remainder: []
```

The calculator we built in this example still has significant shortcomings, the most significant being the fact that you can only use each operator once. We'll remedy this issue in the next chapter, where we will use our parsing library to build a small spreadsheet application.

Case Study: Building a Spreadsheet Application

In this chapter, we'll build a parser, an evaluator, and a GUI for a very simple spreadsheet application. A spreadsheet consists of cells which are organized in rows and columns. Each cell can contain a formula, for example 10*2. As a result of parsing the formula, we construct an *abstract syntax tree*, which is a tree structure that describes the formula. Then we evaluate those formula syntax trees to compute the results for each cell and show them in a table view.

The rows in our spreadsheet are numbered (starting from 0), and the columns are named (from A to Z). The expression C10 refers to the cell in row 10 and column C. An expression in the form of A0:A10 refers to a list of cells. In this case, it is the list of cells starting with the first cell in column A up to (and including) cell 10 in column A.

To build this spreadsheet application, we'll make use of the parsing library we have built in the previous chapter. We've already used it there to build a simple calculator. Now we'll expand on that to parse the slightly more complicated formulas in the spreadsheet: in addition to simple arithmetic operations, they also support references to other cells and functions, like SUM(A0:A10).

Finally, with the functional core of parsing and evaluation in place, we will show how to integrate this pure functional core with the user interface that's written in an object-oriented way using the standard Cocoa frameworks.

Sample Code

Contrary to many of the other chapters, this chapter comes with a sample project[1] instead of a playground, since the project comes with a simple GUI, and a playground would have been over-challenged with the scope of this example anyway. Please open the "Spreadsheet" project to see the whole example in action.

Parsing

We will divide the parsing phase into two steps: tokenization and parsing. The tokenization step (also called lexing or lexical analysis) transforms the input string into a sequence of tokens. In this process, we also deal with removing

---

1 https://github.com/objcio/functional-swift

whitespace, as well as parsing operator symbols and parentheses, so that we do not have to worry about that in our parser.

The second step — parsing — then operates on the sequence of tokens returned by the tokenizer and transforms those into an abstract syntax tree: a tree structure that represents a formula expression.

Tokenization

To produce the list of tokens, we could use the NSScanner class that comes with Apple's Foundation framework. If we want a nice Swift API, we'd have to wrap it first. In addition, we would need to turn off automatic skipping of whitespace and handle whitespace ourselves. Therefore, it is much easier and more instructive in the context of this book to not use NSScanner and instead write a scanner with the parsing library that we have built.

As we do so often when approaching a problem functionally, we first define the Token data type. It's an enum with five cases: numbers, operators, references (such as A10 or C42), punctuation (for now, only parentheses), and function names (such as SUM or AVG):

```
enum Token: Equatable {
    case Number(Int)
    case Operator(String)
    case Reference(String, Int)
    case Punctuation(String)
    case FunctionName(String)
}
```

Now, for each of those cases we'll define parsers, i.e. functions that consume characters from the input string and return a tuple consisting of a token and the remainder of the input string. For example, assuming the formula string 10+2, the parser function for the number case would return the tuple (Token.Number(10), "+2").

But before we jump into this, let's first define a couple of helper functions that will make this code clearer. They might not make too much sense on their own, but please bear with us. You'll see them put to good use in just a moment.

The first of those helper functions is called const and is pretty straightforward:

```
func const<A, B>(x: A) -> (y: B) -> A {
```

```
    return { _ in x }
}
```

You pass a value of type A into const and it returns a constant function, B -> A, i.e. no matter what you pass into the returned function, it will always return what you passed into const in the first place.

Another useful helper is the tokens function. You pass an array of elements into it, and it constructs a parser that will consume exactly those elements from its input and return a tuple consisting of the array you passed in and the remainder of elements left:

```
func tokens<A: Equatable>(input: [A]) -> Parser<A, [A]> {
    guard let (head, tail) = input.decompose else { return pure([]) }
    return prepend </> token(head) <*> tokens(tail)
}
```

If this looks like magic to you, please make sure to read the parser combinators chapter, which explains all the basic building blocks of the parsing library, like the </> and <*> operators.

Using tokens works recursively on the array you pass in: it splits it into its head (the first element) and tail (the remaining elements). Then it parses the head element using the token function we already used in the previous chapter, combined with a recursive call to the tokens function itself on the tail.

With this function in place, we can very easily create a string function that constructs a parser that parses a specific string:

```
func string(string: String) -> Parser<Character, String> {
    return const(string) </> tokens(Array(string.characters))
}
```

Finally, we'll introduce a oneOf helper function that lets us combine multiple parsers in a mutually exclusive manner (for example, we want to parse one of the operators +, -, /, and *):

```
func oneOf<Token, A>(parsers: [Parser<Token, A>]) -> Parser<Token, A> {
    return parsers.reduce(fail(), combine: <|>)
}
```

The fail helper used in the function above simply returns a parser that always fails, no matter what the input is.

With all these helpers in place, let's start with the number case. For this, we define a parser that parses natural numbers by consuming one or more decimal digits from the stream of characters and then combines them into an integer, leveraging the power of the reduce function:

```
let pDigit = oneOf(Array(0...9).map { const($0) </> string("\($0)") })
```

```
func toNaturalNumber(digits: [Int]) -> Int {
    return digits.reduce(0) { $0 * 10 + $1 }
}
```

```
let naturalNumber = toNaturalNumber </> oneOrMore(pDigit)
```

Now we can define a tNumber function that simply parses a natural number and produces a Token by wrapping the parsed number in the Number case:

```
let tNumber = { Token.Number($0) } </> naturalNumber
```

To test the number tokenizer, let's run it on the input "42":

```
parse(tNumber, "42")
```

```
Optional(main.Token.Number(42))
```

Next up are operators: we have to parse the string representing the operator and wrap it in the Token's .Operator case. For each operator that's defined in the array below, we use the string function to convert it into a parser and then combine those parsers for individual operators using the oneOf function:

```
let operatorParsers = ["*", "/", "+", "-", ":"].map { string($0) }
let tOperator = { Token.Operator($0) } </> oneOf(operatorParsers)
```

For references, we have to parse a single capital letter followed by a natural number. First we build a capital parser using the charactersFromSet helper function from the previous chapter:

```
let capitalSet = NSCharacterSet.uppercaseLetterCharacterSet()
let capital = characterFromSet(capitalSet)
```

Now we can use the capital parser in conjunction with the naturalNumber parser to parse a reference. Since we combine two values, we have to curry the function that constructs the reference:

```
let tReference = curry { Token.Reference(String($0), $1) }
```

```
</> capital <*> naturalNumber
```

The punctuation case is very simple as well: it's either an opening parenthesis or a closing parenthesis, which is then wrapped in the Punctuation case:

```
let punctuationParsers = ["(", ")"]. map { string($0) }
let tPunctuation = { Token.Punctuation($0) } </> oneOf(punctuationParsers)
```

Finally, function names (such as SUM) consist of one or more capital letters, which are converted into a string and wrapped in the FunctionName case:

```
let tName = { Token.FunctionName(String($0)) } </> oneOrMore(capital)
```

Now we have all the functions in place to generate a stream of tokens for our formula expressions. Since we want to ignore any kind of whitespace in those formulas, we define one more helper function, ignoreLeadingWhitespace, that 'eats up' whitespace between tokens:

```
let whitespaceSet = NSCharacterSet.whitespaceAndNewlineCharacterSet()
let whitespace = characterFromSet(whitespaceSet)

func ignoreLeadingWhitespace<A>(p: Parser<Character, A>)
    -> Parser<Character, A>
{
    return zeroOrMore(whitespace) *> p
}
```

The complete expression parser can now be defined as a combination of all the parsers above with the oneOf function, wrapped with the ignoreLeadingWhitespace function to dispose of whitespace, and finally wrapped with the zeroOrMore function to make sure we get a list of tokens back:

```
func tokenize() -> Parser<Character, [Token]> {
    let tokenParsers = [tNumber, tOperator, tReference, tPunctuation, tName]
    return zeroOrMore(ignoreLeadingWhitespace(oneOf(tokenParsers)))
}
```

That's all there is to the tokenizer. Now we can run it on a sample expression:

```
parse(tokenize(), "1+2*3+SUM(A4:A6)")

Optional([main.Token.Number(1), main.Token.Operator("+"),
main.Token.Number(2), main.Token.Operator("*"), main.Token.Number(3),
```

```
main.Token.Operator("+"), main.Token.FunctionName("SUM"),
main.Token.Punctuation("("), main.Token.Reference("A", 4),
main.Token.Operator(":"), main.Token.Reference("A", 6),
main.Token.Punctuation(")")])
```

Parsing

From the list of tokens generated by our tokenizer, we now create an expression. Expressions can be either numbers, references (to another cell), binary expressions with an operator, or function calls. We can capture that in the following recursive enum, which is the abstract syntax tree for spreadsheet expressions:

```
indirect enum Expression {
    case Number(Int)
    case Reference(String, Int)
    case BinaryExpression(String, Expression, Expression)
    case FunctionCall(String, Expression)
}
```

So far, we have only constructed parsers that work on strings (or to be more precise, a list of characters). However, we have defined our parsers in such a way that they can work on any type of tokens, including the Token type we have defined above.

First, we define a simple type alias for our parser, which says that it computes Expression values out of a stream of Token values:

```
typealias ExpressionParser = Parser<Token, Expression>
```

Let's start with parsing numbers. When trying to parse a token to a number expression, two things can happen: either the parsing succeeds in case the token was a number token, or it fails for all other cases. To construct our number parser, we'll define a helper function, optionalTransform, that lets us transform the parsed token to an expression, or return **nil** in case the token can't be transformed into a number expression:

```
func optionalTransform<A, T>(f: T -> A?) -> Parser<T, A> {
    return { f($0)! } </> satisfy { f($0) != nil }
}
```

Now we can define the number parser. Note that the Number case is used twice: the first instance is the Token.Number case, and the second instance is the Expression.Number case:

```
let pNumber: ExpressionParser = optionalTransform {
    guard case let .Number(number) = $0 else { return nil }
    return Expression.Number(number)
}
```

Parsing references is equally simple:

```
let pReference: ExpressionParser = optionalTransform {
    guard case let .Reference(column, row) = $0 else { return nil }
    return Expression.Reference(column, row)
}
```

Finally, we combine those two into one parser:

```
let pNumberOrReference = pNumber <|> pReference
```

We can now apply this parser to both numbers and references to see that it works as expected:

```
parse(pNumberOrReference, parse(tokenize(), "42")!)
```

```
Optional(main.Expression.Number(42))
```

```
parse(pNumberOrReference, parse(tokenize(), "A5")!)
```

```
Optional(main.Expression.Reference("A", 5))
```

Next, let's take a look at function calls such as SUM(...). In order to do that, we first define a parser, similar to the number and reference parsers above, that parses a function name token or returns nil if the token is not of type Token.FunctionName:

```
let pFunctionName: Parser<Token, String> = optionalTransform {
    guard case let .FunctionName(name) = $0 else { return nil }
    return name
}
```

In our case, the argument of a function call is always a list of cell references in the form of A1:A3. The list parser has to parse two reference tokens separated by a : operator token:

```
func makeList(l: Expression, _ r: Expression) -> Expression {
    return Expression.BinaryExpression(":", l, r)
}
```

```
let pList: ExpressionParser = curry(makeList)
    </> pReference <* op(":") <*> pReference
```

op is a simple helper that takes an operator string and creates a parser that parses a corresponding operator token, returning the operator string as a result:

```
func op(opString: String) -> Parser<Token, String> {
    return const(opString) </> token(Token.Operator(opString))
}
```

Before we can put everything together to parse a function call, we still need a function to parse a parenthesized expression:

```
func parenthesized<A>(p: Parser<Token, A>) -> Parser<Token, A> {
    return token(Token.Punctuation("(")) *> p <* token(Token.Punctuation(")"))
}
```

This function takes any parser p as argument and combines it with a parser for an opening parenthesis on the left, and one for a closing parenthesis on the right. The result of parenthesized is the same as the result of parsing p, since the parentheses get thrown away due to the use of the *> and <* combinator operators.

Now we can combine all those elements to parse a complete function call:

```
func makeFunctionCall(name: String, _ arg: Expression) -> Expression {
    return Expression.FunctionCall(name, arg)
}
```

```
let pFunctionCall = curry(makeFunctionCall)
    </> pFunctionName <*> parenthesized(pList)
```

Let's give it a try:

```
parse(pFunctionCall, parse(tokenize(), "SUM(A1:A3)")!)
```

```
Optional(main.Expression.FunctionCall("SUM",
main.Expression.BinaryExpression(":", main.Expression.Reference("A",
1), main.Expression.Reference("A", 3))))
```

To parse whole formula expressions, we have to start with the smallest building blocks that expressions consist of and work our way outward to respect operator precedence. For example, we want to parse multiplications with higher precedence than additions. To start with, we define a parser for formula primitives:

```
let pParenthesizedExpression = parenthesized(lazy { expression() })
let pPrimitive = pNumberOrReference <|> pFunctionCall
    <|> pParenthesizedExpression
```

A primitive is either a number, a reference, a function call, or another expression wrapped in brackets. For the latter, we need to use the **lazy** helper function, which ensures that expressionParser only gets called if it really needs to be, otherwise we would get stuck in an endless loop.

Now that we can parse primitives, we'll put them together to parse products (or divisions for that matter — we'll treat them as equal, as they have the same operator precedence). A product consists of at least one factor, followed by zero or more * factor or / factor pairs. Those pairs can be modeled as the following:

```
let pMultiplier = curry { ($0, $1) } </> (op("*") <|> op("/")) <*> pPrimitive
```

The result of the pMultiplier parser is a tuple consisting of the operator string (e.g. "*") and the expression to its right. Consequently, the whole product parser looks like this:

```
let pProduct = curry(combineOperands) </> pPrimitive <*> zeroOrMore(pMultiplier)
```

The key here is the combineOperands function, which builds an expression tree from one primitive and zero or more multiplier tuples. We have to make sure to respect the operator's left associativity when building this tree (it doesn't matter for *, since it is commutative, but it does for /). Luckily, reduce works in a left-associative manner, i.e. a sequence like 1, 2, 3, 4 is reduced in the order (((1, 2), 3), 4). We leverage this behavior to combine multiple operands into one expression:

```
func combineOperands(first: Expression, _ rest: [(String, Expression)])
    -> Expression
{
    return rest.reduce(first) { result, pair in
        let (op, exp) = pair
        return Expression.BinaryExpression(op, result, exp)
```

204 Case Study: Building a Spreadsheet Application

```
    }
}
```

Now we can parse primitives and products of primitives. The last missing piece in the puzzle is the addition of one or more of those products. Since this follows exactly the same pattern as the product itself, we'll keep it brief:

```
let pSummand = curry { ($0, $1) } </> (op("-") <|> op("+")) <*> pProduct
let pSum = curry(combineOperands) </> pProduct <*> zeroOrMore(pSummand)
```

A whole formula expression can now be parsed by the pSum parser. We alias it as expression:

```
expression = { pSum }
```

Now we combine our tokenizer and parser into a function, parseExpression. It first tokenizes the input string, and then — if this succeeds — it parses the expression:

```
func parseExpression(input: String) -> Expression? {
    return parse(tokenize(), input).flatMap { parse(expression(), $0) }
}
```

Applying this function to a complete formula yields the expression tree as we would expect:

```
parseExpression("1 + 2*3 - MIN(A5:A9)")
```

```
Optional(main.Expression.BinaryExpression("-",
main.Expression.BinaryExpression("+", main.Expression.Number(1),
main.Expression.BinaryExpression("*", main.Expression.Number(2),
main.Expression.Number(3))), main.Expression.FunctionCall("MIN",
main.Expression.BinaryExpression(":", main.Expression.Reference("A",
5), main.Expression.Reference("A", 9)))))
```

Evaluation

Now that we have an abstract syntax tree (in the form of Expression values), we can evaluate these expressions into results. For our simple example, we will assume a one-dimensional spreadsheet (i.e. with only one column). It's not too hard to extend the example into a two-dimensional spreadsheet, but for explanatory purposes, sticking to one dimension makes things clearer.

In order to make the code easier to read, we'll make another simplification: we don't cache the results of evaluating cell expressions. In a 'real' spreadsheet, it would be important to define the order of operations. For example, if cell A2 uses the value of A1, it is useful to first compute A1 and cache that result, so that we can use the cached result when computing A2's value. Adding this is not hard, but we leave it as an exercise for the reader for the sake of clarity.

That said, let's start by defining our Result enum. When we evaluate an expression, there are three different possible results. In the case of simple arithmetic expressions such as 10+10, the result will be a number, which is covered by the case IntResult. In the case of an expression like A0:A10, the result is a list of results, which is covered by the case ListResult. Finally, it is very possible that there is an error, for example, when an expression can't be parsed, or when an illegal expression is used. In this case, we want to display an error, which is covered by the EvaluationError case:

```
enum Result {
    case IntResult(Int)
    case StringResult(String)
    case ListResult([Result])
    case EvaluationError(String)
}
```

Before we continue with the evaluation, we first define a helper function called lift . It makes it possible for us to use functions that normally work on integers to work on the Result enum. For example, the + operator is a function that takes two integers and sums them up. Using lift , we can lift the + operator into a function that takes two Result values, and if both are IntResults, it combines them into a new IntResult. If either of the Result values is not an IntResult, the function returns an evaluation error:

```
typealias IntegerOperator = (Int, Int) -> Int

func lift (f: IntegerOperator) -> ((Result, Result) -> Result) {
    return { l, r in
        guard case let (.IntResult(x), .IntResult(y)) = (l, r) else {
            return .EvaluationError("Couldn't evaluate \(l, r)")
        }
        return .IntResult(f(x, y))
    }
}
```

Our tokenizer supports the "+", "/", "*", and "-" operators. However, in our expression enum, there's the BinaryExpression case, which stores the operator as a String value. Therefore, we need a way to map those strings into functions that combine two Ints. We define a dictionary, integerOperators, which captures exactly that:

```
let integerOperators: [String: IntegerOperator] = [
    "+": op(+),
    "/": op (/),
    "*": op(*),
    "-": op(-)
]
```

Now we can write a function, evaluateIntegerOperator, that, given an operator string op and two expressions, returns a result. As an additional parameter, it gets a function, evaluate, which knows how to evaluate an expression:

```
func evaluateIntegerOperator(op: String, _ l: Expression, _ r: Expression,
    _ evaluate: Expression? -> Result) -> Result?
{
    return integerOperators[op].map {
        lift ($0)(evaluate(l),  evaluate(r))
    }
}
```

The operator op is looked up in the integerOperators dictionary, which returns an optional function with type (Int, Int) -> Int. We use the map on optionals and then evaluate the left argument and the right argument, giving us two results. We finally use the lift function to combine the two results into a new result. Note that if the operator couldn't be recognized, this returns **nil**.

To evaluate the list operator (e.g. A1:A5), we define evaluateListOperator, similar to evaluateIntegerOperator above:

```
func evaluateListOperator(op: String, _ l:  Expression, _ r: Expression,
    _ evaluate: Expression? -> Result) -> Result?
{
    switch (op, l,  r) {
    case (":",  .Reference("A", let row1), .Reference("A", let row2))
        where row1 <= row2:
        return Result.ListResult(Array(row1...row2).map {
            evaluate(Expression.Reference("A", $0))
        })
    default:
```

```
        return nil
    }
}
```

We first check if the operator string is actually the list operator :. Also, because we only support one column, we want to make sure that both l and r are references and that row2 is larger than or equal to row1. Note that we can check all of those conditions at the same time using a single switch case; in all other cases, we simply return **nil**. In the case that all our preconditions are fulfilled, we map over each cell and evaluate the result.

Now we're ready to evaluate any binary operator. First, we try if the integer operator succeeds. In case this returns **nil**, we try to evaluate the list operator. In case that also doesn't succeed, we return an error:

```
func evaluateBinary(op: String, _ l: Expression, _ r: Expression,
    _ evaluate: Expression? -> Result) -> Result
{
    return evaluateIntegerOperator(op, l, r, evaluate)
        ?? evaluateListOperator(op, l, r, evaluate)
        ?? .EvaluationError("Couldn't find operator \(op)")
}
```

For now, we'll support two functions on lists, SUM and MIN, which compute the sum and the minimum of a list, respectively. Given a function name and the result of the parameter (we currently only support functions with exactly one parameter), we switch on the function name and check in both cases if the parameter is a list result. If yes, we simply compute the sum or the minimum of the results. Because these lists are not lists with Ints, but rather lists with Results, we need to lift the operator using the lift function:

```
func evaluateFunction(functionName: String, _ parameter: Result) -> Result {
    switch (functionName, parameter) {
    case ("SUM", .ListResult(let list )):
        return list .reduce(Result.IntResult(0), combine: lift(+))
    case ("MIN", .ListResult(let list )):
        return list .reduce(Result.IntResult(Int.max),
            combine: lift { min($0, $1) })
    default:
        return .EvaluationError("Couldn't evaluate function")
    }
}
```

We finally have all the pieces together to evaluate a single expression. In order to do this, we also need all other expressions (because the expression might reference another cell). Therefore, the evaluateExpression function takes a context argument that is an array of optional expressions: one for each cell (the first element in the array is A0, the second A1, and so on). In case parsing failed, the optional expression has a **nil** value. All that evaluateExpression does is switch on the expression and call the appropriate evaluation functions:

```
func evaluateExpression(context: [Expression?]) -> Expression? -> Result {
    return { (e: Expression?) in
        e.map { expression in
            let recurse = evaluateExpression(context)
            switch (expression) {
            case let .Number(x):
                return Result.IntResult(x)
            case let .Reference("A", idx):
                return recurse(context[idx])
            case let .BinaryExpression(s, l, r):
                return evaluateBinary(s, l, r, recurse)
            case let .FunctionCall(f, p):
                return evaluateFunction(f, recurse(p))
            default:
                return .EvaluationError("Couldn't evaluate expression")
            }
        } ?? .EvaluationError("Couldn't parse expression")
    }
}
```

Finally, we can define a convenience function, evaluateExpressions, which takes a list of optional expressions, and produces a list of results by mapping evaluateExpression over it:

```
func evaluateExpressions(expressions: [Expression?]) -> [Result] {
    return expressions.map(evaluateExpression(expressions))
}
```

As stated in the introduction of this chapter and throughout the text, there are a lot of limitations to the current parser and evaluator. There could be better error messages, a dependency analysis of the cells, loop detection, massive optimizations, and much more. But note that we have defined the entire model layer of a spreadsheet, parsing, and evaluation in about 200 lines. This is the power of functional programming: after thinking about the types and data structures, many of the functions are fairly straightforward to write. And once the code is written, we can always make it better and faster.

Furthermore, we were able to reuse many of the standard library functions within our expression language. The lift combinator made it really simple to reuse any binary function that works on integers. We were able to compute the results of functions like SUM and MIN using reduce. And with the parsing library from the previous chapter in place, we quickly wrote both a lexer and a parser.

The GUI

Now that we have the formula parser and evaluator in place, we can build a simple GUI around them. Because almost all frameworks in Cocoa are object oriented, we'll have to mix OOP and functional programming to get this working. Luckily, Swift makes that really easy.

We will create an XIB containing our window, which contains a single NSTableView with one column. The table view is populated by a data source and has a delegate to handle the editing. Both the data source and delegate are separate objects. The data source stores the formulas and their results, and the delegate tells the data source which row is currently being edited. The edited row is then displayed as a formula rather than a result.

The Data Source

Our data source is exactly where the functional and OOP parts mix. It is an object that conforms to the NSTableViewDataSource protocol, which provides the data for an NSTableView. In our case, the data is the cells. Depending on whether a cell is currently being edited, we display either the formula (when edited), or the result. In our class, we need to store the formulas, the computed results, and the row that is currently being edited (which might be **nil**):

```
class SpreadsheetDatasource: NSObject, NSTableViewDataSource, EditedRow {
    var formulas: [String]
    var results: [Result]
    var editedRow: Int? = nil
    // ...
}
```

In this class's initializer, we initialize the formulas with strings representing the numbers one to ten. We also initialize the results of these formulas with the corresponding values:

```
override init () {
    let initialValues = Array(1..<10)
    formulas = initialValues.map { "\($0)" }
    results = initialValues.map { Result.IntResult($0) }
}
```

The table view's delegate protocol requires us to implement two methods: the first method returns the number of rows in the table view (which is simply the number of formulas). The second method returns the content for each cell. In our case, we look at the row, and if it's the row that's currently being edited, we return the formula. Otherwise, we return the result:

```
func numberOfRowsInTableView(tableView: NSTableView) -> Int {
    return formulas.count
}
```

```
func tableView(aTableView: NSTableView,
    objectValueForTableColumn: NSTableColumn?, row: Int) -> AnyObject?
{
    return editedRow == row ? formulas[row] : results[row].description
}
```

When the user has edited a cell, we reevaluate all formulas:

```
func tableView(aTableView: NSTableView, setObjectValue: AnyObject?,
    forTableColumn: NSTableColumn?, row: Int)
{
    let string = setObjectValue as! String
    formulas[row] = string
    calculateExpressions()
    aTableView.reloadData()
}
```

In order to calculate expressions, we map over each formula to tokenize and parse it. We use the parseExpression function defined earlier. This will return a list of optional expressions (in case either tokenization or parsing has failed). Then, we use the evaluate function to compute a list of results:

```
func calculateExpressions() {
    results = evaluateExpressions(formulas.map(parseExpression))
}
```

The Delegate

The delegate's only task is to let the data source know which cell is currently being edited. Because we'd like a loose coupling between the two, we'll introduce an extra protocol, EditedRow, which describes that there should be a property, editedRow, which optionally contains the value of the row that's currently being edited (you might have already noticed this protocol in the declaration of the SpreadsheetDatasource class):

```
protocol EditedRow {
    var editedRow: Int? { get set }
}
```

Now, when the row is edited, we just set that property on the data source and we're done:

```
class SpreadsheetDelegate: NSObject, NSTableViewDelegate {
    var editedRowDelegate: EditedRow?

    func tableView(aTableView: NSTableView,
        shouldEditTableColumn aTableColumn: NSTableColumn?,
        row rowIndex: Int) -> Bool
    {
        editedRowDelegate?.editedRow = rowIndex
        return true
    }
}
```

The Window Controller

The final bit that ties everything together is the window controller. (If you come from iOS, this fulfills a similar role as UIViewController does.) The window controller has outlets to the table view, the data source, and the delegate. All of these objects are instantiated by the nib file:

```
class SheetWindowController: NSWindowController {

    @IBOutlet var tableView: NSTableView! = nil
    @IBOutlet var dataSource: SpreadsheetDatasource?
    @IBOutlet var delegate: SpreadsheetDelegate?
```

When the window loads, we hook up the delegate with the data source so that it can notify the data source about edited rows. Also, we register an observer that will let us know when editing ends. When the notification for the end of editing is fired, we set the data source's edited row to **nil**:

```
override func windowDidLoad() {
    delegate?.editedRowDelegate = dataSource
    NSNotificationCenter.defaultCenter().addObserver(self,
        selector: NSSelectorFromString("endEditing:"),
        name: NSControlTextDidEndEditingNotification, object: nil)
}

func endEditing(note: NSNotification) {
    if  note.object as! NSObject === tableView {
        dataSource?.editedRow = nil
    }
}
}
```

This is all there is to it. We now have a fully working prototype of a single-column spreadsheet. Check out the sample project[2] for the complete example.

Functors, Applicative Functors, and Monads

In this chapter, we will explain some terminology and common patterns used in functional programming, including functors, applicative functors, and monads. Understanding these common patterns will help you design your own data types and choose the correct functions to provide in your APIs.

Functors

Thus far, we have seen three different functions named map, with the following types (curried for brevity):

func map<T, U>(xs: [T])(transform: T -> U) -> [U]
func map<T, U>(**optional**: T?)(transform: T -> U) -> U?
func map<T, U>(result: Result<T>)(transform: T -> U) -> Result<U>

Why have three such different functions with the same name? To answer that question, let's investigate how these functions are related. To begin with, it helps to expand some of the shorthand notation that Swift uses. Optional types, such as Int?, can also be written out explicitly as Optional<Int>, in the same way that we can write Array<T> rather than [T]. If we now state the types of the map function on arrays and optionals, the similarity becomes more apparent:

extension Optional {
    func map<U>(transform: Wrapped -> U) -> Optional<U>
}

extension Array {
    func map<U>(transform: Element -> U) -> Array<U>
}

Both Optional and Array are *type constructors* that expect a generic type argument. For instance, Array<T> and Optional<Int> are valid types, but Array by itself is not. Both of these map functions take two arguments: the structure being mapped, and a function transform of type T -> U. The map functions use a function argument to transform all the values of type T to values of type U in the argument array or optional. Type constructors — such as optionals or arrays — that support a map operation are sometimes referred to as *functors*.

In fact, there are many other types that we have defined that are indeed functors. For example, we can implement a map function on the Result type from Chapter 8:

```
extension Result {
    func map<U>(f: T -> U) -> Result<U> {
        switch self {
        case let .Success(value): return .Success(f(value))
        case let .Error(error):  return .Error(error)
        }
    }
}
```

Similarly, the types we have seen for binary search trees, tries, and parser combinators are all functors. Functors are sometimes described as 'containers' storing values of some type. The map functions transform the stored values stored in a container. This can be a useful intuition, but it can be too restrictive. Remember the Region type that we saw in Chapter 2?

```
typealias Region = Position -> Bool
```

Using this definition of regions, we can only generate black and white bitmaps. We can generalize this to abstract over the kind of information we associate with every position:

```
struct Region<T> {
    let value: Position -> T
}
```

```
extension Region {
    func map<U>(transform: T -> U) -> Region<U> {
        return Region<U> { pos in transform(self.value(pos)) }
    }
}
```

Such regions are a good example of a functor that does not fit well with the intuition of functors being containers. Here, we have represented regions as *functions*, which seem very different from containers.

Almost every generic enumeration that you can define in Swift will be a functor. Providing a map function gives fellow developers a powerful, yet familiar, function for working with such enumerations.

Applicative Functors

Many functors also support other operations aside from map. For example, the parsers from Chapter 12 were not only functors, but also defined the following two operations:

func pure<Token, A>(value: A) -> Parser<Token, A>

func <*><Token, A, B>(l: Parser<Token, A -> B>, r: Parser<Token, A>)
    -> Parser<Token, B>

The pure function explains how to turn any value into a (trivial) parser that returns that value. Meanwhile, the <*> operator sequences two parsers: the first parser returns a function, and the second parser returns an argument for this function. The choice for these two operations is no coincidence. Any type constructor for which we can define appropriate pure and <*> operations is called an *applicative functor*. To be more precise, a functor F is applicative when it supports the following operations:

func pure<A>(value: A) -> F<A>

func <*><A, B>(f: F<A -> B>, x: F<A>) -> F<B>

Applicative functors have been lurking in the background throughout this book. For example, the Region struct defined above is also an applicative functor:

```
func pure<A>(value: A) -> Region<A> {
    return Region { pos in value }
}

func <*><A, B>(regionF: Region<A -> B>, regionX: Region<A>) -> Region<B> {
    return Region { pos in regionF.value(pos)(regionX.value(pos)) }
}
```

Now the pure function always returns a constant value for every region. The <*> operator distributes the position to both its region arguments, which yields a function of type A -> B, and a value of type A. It then combines these in the obvious manner, by applying the resulting function to the argument.

Many of the functions defined on regions can be described succinctly using these two basic building blocks. Here are a few example functions — inspired by Chapter 2 — written in applicative style:

```
func everywhere() -> Region<Bool> {
    return pure(true)
}

func invert(region: Region<Bool>) -> Region<Bool> {
    return pure(!) <*> region
}

func intersection(region1: Region<Bool>, region2: Region<Bool>)
    -> Region<Bool>
{
    let and: Bool -> Bool -> Bool = { x in { y in x && y } }
    return pure(and) <*> region1 <*> region2
}
```

This shows how the applicative instance for the Region type can be used to define pointwise operations on regions.

Applicative functors are not limited to regions and parsers. Swift's built-in optional type is another example of an applicative functor. The corresponding definitions are fairly straightforward:

```
func pure<A>(value: A) -> A? {
    return value
}

func <*><A, B>(optionalTransform: (A -> B)?, optionalValue: A?) -> B? {
    guard let transform = optionalTransform, value = optionalValue
        else { return nil }
    return transform(value)
}
```

The pure function wraps a value into an optional. This is usually handled implicitly by the Swift compiler, so it's not very useful to define ourselves. The <*> operator is more interesting: given a (possibly nil) function and a (possibly nil) argument, it returns the result of applying the function to the argument when both exist. If either argument is nil, the whole function returns nil. We can give similar definitions for pure and <*> for the Result type from Chapter 8.

By themselves, these definitions may not be very interesting, so let's revisit some of our previous examples. You may want to recall the addOptionals function, which tried to add two possibly nil integers:

```
func addOptionals(optionalX: Int?, optionalY: Int?) -> Int? {
```

Functors, Applicative Functors, and Monads   221

```
    guard let x = optionalX, y = optionalY else { return nil }
    return x + y
}
```

Using the definitions above, we can give a short alternative definition of addOptionals using a single **return** statement:

```
func addOptionals(optionalX: Int?, optionalY: Int?) -> Int? {
    return pure(curry(+)) <*> optionalX <*> optionalY
}
```

Once you understand the control flow that operators like <*> encapsulate, it becomes much easier to assemble complex computations in this fashion.

There is one other example from the optionals chapter that we would like to revisit:

```
func populationOfCapital(country: String) -> Int? {
    guard let capital = capitals[country], population = cities[capital]
        else { return nil }
    return population * 1000
}
```

Here we consulted one dictionary, capitals, to retrieve the capital city of a given country. We then consulted another dictionary, cities, to determine each city's population. Despite the obvious similarity to the previous addOptionals example, this function *cannot* be written in applicative style. Here is what happens when we try to do so:

```
func populationOfCapital(country: String) -> Int? {
    return { pop in pop * 1000 } <*> capitals[country] <*> cities [...]
}
```

The problem is that the *result* of the first lookup, which was bound to the capital variable in the original version, is needed in the second lookup. Using only the applicative operations, we quickly get stuck: there is no way for the result of one applicative computation (capitals[country]) to influence another (the lookup in the cities dictionary). To deal with this, we need yet another interface.

The M-Word

In Chapter 5, we gave the following alternative definition of populationOfCapital:

```
func populationOfCapital3(country: String) -> Int? {
    return capitals[country].flatMap { capital in
        return cities [capital]
    }. flatMap { population in
        return population * 1000
    }
}
```

Here we used the built-in flatMap function to combine optional computations. How is this different from the applicative interface? The types are subtly different. In the applicative <*> operation, *both* arguments are optionals. In the flatMap function, on the other hand, the second argument is a *function* that returns an optional value. Consequently, we can pass the result of the first dictionary lookup on to the second.

The flatMap function is impossible to define in terms of the applicative functions. In fact, the flatMap function is one of the two functions supported by *monads*. More generally, a type constructor F is a monad if it defines the following two functions:

```
func pure<A>(value: A) -> F<A>
```

```
func flatMap<A, B>(x: F<A>)(f: A -> F<B>) -> F<B>
```

The flatMap function is sometimes defined as an operator, >>=. This operator is pronounced "bind," as it binds the result of the first argument to the parameter of its second argument.

In addition to Swift's optional type, the Result enumeration defined in Chapter 8 is also a monad. This insight makes it possible to chain together computations that may return an ErrorType. For example, we could define a function that copies the contents of one file to another, as follows:

```
func copyFile(sourcePath: String, targetPath: String, encoding: Encoding)
    -> Result<()>
{
    return readFile(sourcePath, encoding).flatMap { contents in
        writeFile(contents, targetPath, encoding)
```

```
    }
}
```

If the call to either readFile or writeFile fails, the NSError will be logged in the result. This may not be quite as nice as Swift's optional binding mechanism, but it is still pretty close.

There are many other applications of monads aside from handling errors. For example, arrays are also a monad. In the standard library, flatMap is already defined, but you could implement it like this:

```
func pure<A>(value: A) -> [A] {
    return [value]
}


extension Array {
    func flatMap<B>(f: Element -> [B]) -> [B] {
        return self.map(f).reduce([]) { result, xs in result + xs }
    }
}
```

What have we gained from these definitions? The monad structure of arrays provides a convenient way to define various combinatorial functions or solve search problems. For example, suppose we need to compute the *cartesian product* of two arrays, xs and ys. The cartesian product consists of a new array of tuples, where the first component of the tuple is drawn from xs, and the second component is drawn from ys. Using a **for** loop directly, we might write:

```
func cartesianProduct1<A, B>(xs: [A], ys: [B]) -> [(A, B)] {
    var result: [(A, B)] = []
    for x in xs {
        for y in ys {
            result += [(x, y)]
        }
    }
    return result
}
```

We can now rewrite cartesianProduct to use flatMap instead of **for** loops:

```
func cartesianProduct2<A, B>(xs: [A], ys: [B]) -> [(A, B)] {
    return xs.flatMap { x in ys.flatMap { y in [(x, y)] } }
}
```

The flatMap function allows us to take an element x from the first array, xs; next, we take an element y from ys. For each pair of x and y, we return the array [(x, y)]. The flatMap function handles combining all these arrays into one large result.

While this example may seem a bit contrived, the flatMap function on arrays has many important applications. Languages like Haskell and Python support special syntactic sugar for defining lists, called *list comprehensions*. These list comprehensions allow you to draw elements from existing lists and check that these elements satisfy certain properties. They can all be de-sugared into a combination of maps, filters, and flatMap. List comprehensions are very similar to optional binding in Swift, except that they work on lists instead of optionals.

Discussion

Why care about these things? Does it really matter if you know that some type is an applicative functor or a monad? We think it does.

Consider the parser combinators from Chapter 12. Defining the correct way to sequence two parsers is not easy: it requires a bit of insight into how parsers work. Yet it is an absolutely essential piece of our library, without which we could not even write the simplest parsers. If you have the insight that our parsers form an applicative functor, you may realize that the existing <*> provides you with exactly the right notion of sequencing two parsers, one after the other. Knowing what abstract operations your types support can help you find such complex definitions.

Abstract notions, like functors, provide important vocabulary. If you ever encounter a function named map, you can probably make a pretty good guess as to what it does. Without a precise terminology for common structures like functors, you would have to rediscover each new map function from scratch.

These structures give guidance when designing your own API. If you define a generic enumeration or struct, chances are that it supports a map operation. Is this something that you want to expose to your users? Is your data structure also an applicative functor? Is it a monad? What do the operations do? Once you familiarize yourself with these abstract structures, you see them pop up again and again.

Although it is harder in Swift than in Haskell, you can define generic functions that work on any applicative functor. Functions such as the `</>` operator on parsers were defined exclusively in terms of the applicative pure and `<*>` functions. As a result, we may want to redefine them for *other* applicative functors aside from parsers. In this way, we recognize common patterns in how we program using these abstract structures; these patterns may themselves be useful in a wide variety of settings.

The historical development of monads in the context of functional programming is interesting. Initially, monads were developed in a branch of Mathematics known as *category theory*. The discovery of their relevance to Computer Science is generally attributed to Moggi (1991) and later popularized by Wadler (1992a; 1992b). Since then, they have been used by functional languages such as Haskell to contain side effects and I/O (Peyton Jones 2001). Applicative functors were first described by McBride and Paterson (2008), although there were many examples already known. A complete overview of the relation between many of the abstract concepts described in this chapter can be found in the Typeclassopedia (Yorgey 2009).

Conclusion

15

So what is functional programming? Many people (mistakenly) believe functional programming is *only* about programming with higher-order functions, such as map and filter . There is much more to it than that.

In the Introduction, we mentioned three qualities that we believe characterize well-designed functional programs in Swift: modularity, a careful treatment of mutable state, and types. In each of the chapters we have seen, these three concepts pop up again and again.

Higher-order functions can certainly help define some abstractions, such as the Filter type in Chapter 3 or the regions in Chapter 2, but they are a means, not an end. The functional wrapper around the Core Image library we defined provides a type-safe and modular way to assemble complex image filters. Generators and sequences (Chapter 11) help us abstract iteration.

Swift's advanced type system can help catch many errors before your code is even run. Optional types (Chapter 5) mark possible **nil** values as suspicious; generics not only facilitate code reuse, but also allow you to enforce certain safety properties (Chapter 4); and enumerations and structs provide the building blocks to model the data in your domain accurately (Chapters 8 and 9).

Referentially transparent functions are easier to reason about and test. Our QuickCheck library (Chapter 6) shows how we can use higher-order functions to *generate* random unit tests for referentially transparent functions. Swift's careful treatment of value types (Chapter 7) allows you to share data freely within your application without having to worry about it changing unintentionally or unexpectedly.

We can use all these ideas in concert to build powerful domain-specific languages. Our libraries for diagrams (Chapter 10) and parser combinators (Chapter 12) both define a small set of functions, providing the modular building blocks that can be used to assemble solutions to large and difficult problems. Our final case study shows how these domain-specific languages can be used in a complete application (Chapter 13).

Finally, many of the types we have seen share similar functions. In Chapter 14, we show how to group them and how they relate to each other.

Further Reading

One way to further hone your functional programming skills is by learning Haskell. There are many other functional languages, such as F#, OCaml, Standard ML, Scala, or Racket, each of which would make a fine choice of language to complement Swift. Haskell, however, is the most likely to challenge your preconceptions about programming. Learning to program well in Haskell will change the way you work in Swift.

There are a lot of Haskell books and courses available these days. Graham Hutton's *Programming in Haskell* (2007) is a great starting point to familiarize yourself with the language basics. *Learn You a Haskell for Great Good!* is free to read online and covers some more advanced topics. *Real World Haskell* describes several larger case studies and a lot of the technology missing from many other books, including support for profiling, debugging, and automated testing. Richard Bird is famous for his "functional pearls" — elegant, instructive examples of functional programming, many of which can be found in his book, *Pearls of Functional Algorithm Design* (2010), or online[1]. Finally, *The Fun of Programming* is a collection of domain-specific languages embedded in Haskell, covering domains ranging from financial contracts to hardware design (Gibbons and de Moor 2003).

If you want to learn more about programming language design in general, Benjamin Pierce's *Types and Programming Languages* (2002) is an obvious choice. Bob Harper's *Practical Foundations for Programming Languages* (2012) is more recent and more rigorous, but unless you have a solid background in computer science or mathematics, you may find it hard going.

Don't feel obliged to make use of all of these resources; many of them may not be of interest to you. But you should be aware that there is a huge amount of work on programming language design, functional programming, and mathematics that has directly influenced the design of Swift.

If you're interested in further developing your Swift skills – not only the functional parts of it – we've written an entire book about advanced swift topics[2], covering topics low-level programming to high-level abstractions.

---

1 http://www.haskell.org/haskellwiki/Research_papers/Functional_pearls
2 https://objc.io/books/advanced-swift

Closure

This is an exciting time for Swift. The language is still very much in its infancy.
Compared to Objective-C, there are many new features — borrowed from
existing functional programming languages — that have the potential to
dramatically change the way we write software for iOS and OS X.

At the same time, it is unclear how the Swift community will develop. Will
people embrace these features? Or will they write the same code in Swift as
they do in Objective-C, but without the semicolons? Time will tell. By writing
this book, we hope to have introduced you to some concepts from functional
programming. It is up to you to put these ideas in practice as we continue to
shape the future of Swift.

Bibliography

Barendregt, H.P. 1984. *The Lambda Calculus, Its Syntax and Semantics*. Studies in Logic and the Foundations of Mathematics. Elsevier.

Bird, Richard. 2010. *Pearls of Functional Algorithm Design*. Cambridge University Press.

Church, Alonzo. 1941. *The Calculi of Lambda-Conversion*. Princeton University Press.

Claessen, Koen, and John Hughes. 2000. "QuickCheck: A Lightweight Tool for Random Testing of Haskell Programs." In *ACM SIGPLAN Notices*, 268–79. ACM Press. doi:http://doi.org/10.1145/357766.351266.

Gibbons, Jeremy, and Oege de Moor, eds. 2003. *The Fun of Programming*. Palgrave Macmillan.

Girard, Jean-Yves. 1972. "Interprétation Fonctionelle et élimination Des Coupures de L'arithmétique d'ordre Supérieur." PhD thesis, Université Paris VII.

Harper, Robert. 2012. *Practical Foundations for Programming Languages*. Cambridge University Press.

Hinze, Ralf, and Ross Paterson. 2006. "Finger Trees: A Simple General-Purpose Data Structure." *Journal of Functional Programming* 16 (02). Cambridge Univ Press: 197–217. doi:http://doi.org/10.1017/S0956796805005769.

Hudak, P., and M.P. Jones. 1994. "Haskell Vs. Ada Vs. C++ Vs. Awk Vs. . an Experiment in Software Prototyping Productivity." Research Report YALEU/DCS/RR-1049. New Haven, CT: Department of Computer Science, Yale University.

Hutton, Graham. 2007. *Programming in Haskell*. Cambridge University Press.

McBride, Conor, and Ross Paterson. 2008. "Applicative Programming with Effects." *Journal of Functional Programming* 18 (01). Cambridge Univ Press: 1–13.

Moggi, Eugenio. 1991. "Notions of Computation and Monads." *Information and Computation* 93 (1). Elsevier: 55–92.

Okasaki, C. 1999. *Purely Functional Data Structures*. Cambridge University Press.

Peyton Jones, Simon. 2001. "Tackling the Awkward Squad: Monadic Input/output, Concurrency, Exceptions, and Foreign-Language Calls in Haskell." In *Engineering Theories of Software Construction*, edited by Tony Hoare, Manfred Broy, and Ralf Steinbruggen, 180:47. IOS Press.

Pierce, Benjamin C. 2002. *Types and Programming Languages*. MIT press.

Reynolds, John C. 1974. "Towards a Theory of Type Structure." In *Programming Symposium*, edited by B.Robinet, 19:408–25. Lecture Notes in Computer Science. Springer.

———. 1983. "Types, Abstraction and Parametric Polymorphism." *Information Processing*.

Strachey, Christopher. 2000. "Fundamental Concepts in Programming Languages." *Higher-Order and Symbolic Computation* 13 (1-2). Springer: 11–49.

Swierstra, S Doaitse. 2009. "Combinator Parsing: A Short Tutorial." In *Language Engineering and Rigorous Software Development*, 252–300. Springer. doi:http://doi.org/10.1.1.184.7953.

Wadler, Philip. 1989. "Theorems for Free!" In *Proceedings of the Fourth International Conference on Functional Programming Languages and Computer Architecture*, 347–59.

———. 1992a. "Comprehending Monads." *Mathematical Structures in Computer Science* 2 (04). Cambridge Univ Press: 461–93.

———. 1992b. "The Essence of Functional Programming." In *POPL '92: Conference Record of the Nineteenth Annual ACM SIGPLAN-SIGACT Symposium on Principles of Programming Languages*, 1–14. ACM.

Yorgey, Brent. 2009. "The Typeclassopedia." *The Monad. Reader* 13: 17.

Yorgey, Brent A. 2012. "Monoids: Theme and Variations (Functional Pearl)." In *Proceedings of the 2012 Haskell Symposium*, 105–16. Haskell '12. Copenhagen, Denmark. doi:http://doi.org/10.1145/2364506.2364520.

CPSIA information can be obtained
at www.ICGtesting.com
Printed in the USA
LVOW04s2256230116

471992LV00019B/1363/P